ACCLAIM FOR *HUNTING THE HUNTERS*

As the rest of the world stood by and watched, Laurens risked everything to defend these extraordinary mammals from extinction. A truly powerful and inspiring story.

Susan Sarandon, Oscar-winning actress and activist

It's risky business putting yourself between whale and harpoon but someone's got to do it! Gripping, real-life adventure from a crewmember who served in the Whales' Navy. Reading of the cold, the ice, the enemy, and the whales who got away, you are there with the Sea Shepherd crew.

Ingrid Newkirk, co-founder and president of PETA

You can't help but admire the sheer determination, unremitting spirit and extraordinary courage of De Groot and his fellow activists. A terrific and eye-opening book about life on the frontline and the people who risk everything in their desperate bid to stop the atrocities of commercial whaling.

Mark Carwardine, zoologist, conservationist, presenter,
photographer and writer

The vast majority of people in the world make up the force that is driving species extinct not by the day but by the hour. Yet in spite of terrible odds and difficult conditions there is a small and dedicated number of people who are working selflessly to stem the rising tide of extinction. Laurens de Groot is one of them. Read his book and you will learn what it takes to lend a hand to reverse the extinction crisis, Mother of All Crises, and you will be inspired to activism.

Douglas Tompkins, conservationist and founder of outdoor brand
The North Face

An insightful and heartbreaking account of the daring crusades against illegal whalers. Shocking and utterly gripping, this books shows how one person can make a difference, and just how important that difference can be.

Isabel Lucas, actress and environmental activist

The vast majority of people on this planet, whether they realise it or not, are living by killing. That's the primal image of life, with humankind and its casual killing – of each other, the environment, animals, insects. And yet, there are also people on this planet who have evolved beyond this primal image of life, wherein living by killing has been transformed into living by loving. Such is the author of the book that you now hold in your hands.

Shaun Monson, writer/director of Earthlings,
winner of Best Documentary Film at San Diego Film Festival

HUNTING THE
HUNTERS

Laurens De Groot

HUNTING THE HUNTERS

AT WAR WITH THE WHALERS

ADLARD COLES NAUTICAL

B L O O M S B U R Y

LONDON • NEW DELHI • NEW YORK • SYDNEY

Published by Adlard Coles Nautical
an imprint of Bloomsbury Publishing Plc
50 Bedford Square, London WC1B 3DP
www.adlardcoles.com

Copyright © 2012 Laurens de Groot. Originally published as *Jacht op de jagers*
by Uitgeverij Thomas Rap, Amsterdam.

English translation © by Laura Vroomen 2014

First published by Adlard Coles Nautical in 2014

ISBN 978-1-4729-0364-8
ePDF 978-1-4729-0366-2
ePub 978-1-4729-0365-5

The right of the author to be identified as the author of this work has been asserted
by him in accordance with the Copyright, Designs and Patents Act, 1988.

A CIP catalogue record for this book is available from the British Library.

This book is produced using paper that is made from wood grown in managed,
sustainable forests. It is natural, renewable and recyclable. The logging and
manufacturing processes conform to the environmental regulations of the country
of origin.

Typeset in 11.25 pt Haarlemmer by Saxon Graphics Ltd, Derby
Printed and bound in Great Britain by CPI Group (UK) Ltd, Croydon CR0 4YY

Note: while all reasonable care has been taken in the publication of this book,
the publisher takes no responsibility for the use of the methods or products
described in the book.

Every effort has been made to obtain permission from copyright holders of
materials included in this book.

10 9 8 7 6 5 4 3 2 1

CONTENTS

Prologue   xi

I   The Mission   **1**

01   Death Without Warning   2
02   Pieces of the Puzzle   9
03   The Last Drop   16
04   Farewell   19
05   Freeing Chickens   24
06   Seasickness   31
07   The First Whale   36
08   Crazy Ivan   45
09   Gotcha!   50
10   Coastguard and Stun Grenades   54
11   The Beggars of Antarctica   59

II   The Adventure   **63**

12   Kung fu in Melbourne   64
13   Room for Three   67
14   Sea Shepherd Samurai   70
15   Fire on Board?   74
16   Ice, Ice Everywhere   79
17   Man Overboard   85
18   Tora, Tora, Huh?   89

19	The Big Bang	99
20	Result!	102
21	This Far and No Further	108
22	On Collision Course!	113
23	Farewell, Antarctica	117
24	Rock 'n' Roll USA	119

III The Expedition   **133**

25	The Doomed Forest	134
26	The Batmobile	140
27	The Gilbillies	146
28	Bazookas and Lasers	152
29	The Calm Before the Devastating Storm	159
30	Rammed!	168
31	Home Sweet Home	177

IV The Forgotten Hunt   **181**

32	This Is Africa	182
33	Operation Desert Seal	189
34	The Factory from Hell	195
35	Warships off the Coast	200
36	Escape Through the Desert	205
37	Spies and Traitors	214
38	In Conclusion	219

Epilogue	221
Acknowledgements	225
Glossary	228

Some of the names in this book have been changed in the interests of privacy.

PROLOGUE

In this atrocious weather Captain Watson's order sounds insane. Yet none of the Sea Shepherd crew kicks up a fuss. Now is not the time for discussion. Now is the time for action. The skipper has just caught sight of the harpoon ship, and we have to do as he says. Right now.

Everybody rushes to take up their assigned positions. Crane operator Arne Feuerhahn starts up the hydraulic crane, while the other deckhands roll out the lines and prepare the dinghies. It will take at least another 15 minutes before everything is ready, and I'm expected on deck to go after the Japanese hunter.

The door to my cabin is locked. Nobody is to disturb me; this action requires total concentration. I look in the mirror above the washbasin. Dilated pupils stare back at me, at my skin, which is paler than usual. My hands are clammy, my mouth is dry and my muscles are so tense I feel like shitting and vomiting at the same time.

A sip of tepid water from the rusty tap does nothing to quell my nerves. I splash a little water on my face and massage my eye sockets with my fingertips. It relaxes me briefly. That's as much as I can do for my physical discomforts. Now it's all down to action. No more thinking, only doing what I've been practising these past 10 days: stopping the Japanese whaling fleet.

My gear is lying on the bench in the cabin: wetsuit, thick woollen socks, Mustang survival coverall, full-face helmet, waterproof shoes, a serrated knife, ski goggles, two pairs of gloves and a survival kit. I put the wetsuit on over my underpants, the only base layer needed.

The neoprene suit is tight and uncomfortable, but these preparations are geared to an emergency in the ice-cold waters of Antarctica. And in those waters a wetsuit can mean the difference between life and death.

Over this base layer I wear the survival coverall, which resembles a space suit. The clothing severely restricts my freedom of movement, but it has two important benefits: it's warm and it floats. Besides, the tight-fitting sleeves keep water out for quite some time. Fall overboard in the Southern Ocean and the combination of coverall and wetsuit gives you about an hour before hypothermia sets in – hopefully just long enough for a rescue attempt by a passing ship.

Finally, I put on my waterproof climbing boots. They're made of Gore-tex, not leather. Not only is the food on all Sea Shepherd vessels vegan; so, ideally, is your clothing. It's not compulsory, but certainly advisable if you want to remain on good terms with the hardcore activists on the ship.

After checking my outfit one last time, I plug in my iPod. There's a ritual to be done before I make my way to the weather deck.

Some 30 minutes before Captain Watson's order, the officers on the bridge first noticed the green dot. Most dots are icebergs, but this one kept moving on the colossal marine radar, which I suspect is a Cold War relic. It has to be another vessel. According to the quartermasters' calculations it's about 6 sea miles away. In the daytime that's normally close enough for us to make out the unknown ship, but today heavy fog banks have reduced visibility to about 2 miles. On the radar we can see the mysterious vessel is sailing parallel to the *Steve Irwin*, our Sea Shepherd ship. And it's gradually coming closer.

As for the identity of the blinking dot, there are a few options: a cruise ship carrying tourists to the South Pole for €6,000 per person; a fishing boat that's probably poaching Antarctic toothfish; or a supply ship. The latter seems unlikely, though, because those vessels don't put out to sea until the end of the Antarctic summer. And then of course there's the option we're hoping for: a Japanese whaler.

The size of the dot suggests we're dealing with a small vessel. That's to say, not as big as the *Nisshin Maru*, the whaling fleet's gigantic factory ship on which harpooned whales are cut to pieces and frozen. It could be a harpoon ship or a spotter ship. If it's the latter, it's probably here on its own, because the spotters scour the ice boundaries hundreds of miles from the fleet, searching for pods of resting whales. As soon as they find minke whales or fin whales, the harpoon and factory ships make their way over and the slaughter commences. But the crew on the bridge is hoping for a harpoon ship. And for good reason: eliminating a hunter is the pinnacle of whale protection.

Rumours about the approaching vessel spread through the Sea Shepherd ship like wildfire. Every bit of news creates a moment of excitement, breaking the dull, daily grind of cleaning, maintenance and cooking. When the news reaches me in the communal dining area, the approaching dot has blown up into the complete whaling fleet and 60 samurai. I decide to take a look on the bridge.

About half the crew have their noses pressed against the windows in the hope of catching a glimpse of the approaching danger. The glass is steaming up. It's getting on Peter Hammarstedt's nerves. With sweeping gestures and in no uncertain terms, the duty officer tells everyone who's not on duty to leave the bridge. Nobody makes a move. Sea Shepherd volunteers are not well-trained marines slavishly obeying orders. Peter has to repeat his request several times before nearly everyone leaves, albeit reluctantly.

I'm allowed to stick around for a while. If the unknown vessel turns out to be a harpoon ship, I'm supposed to go out on the water, and it goes without saying that I want to steal a glance at my opponent. And I also want to have a good look at the surroundings, to see if there are any icebergs we can navigate by in case our equipment fails. And I'm trying to read the weather, which is anything but friendly at the moment. From behind her computer with digital weather maps, quartermaster Jane Taylor, a former US navy officer, predicts that the wind will die down soon. Launching rubber boats won't be a problem, she assures me. But my gut feeling tells me Jane could be wrong. The wind is fluctuating between force 3 and 5, with scattered whitecaps on the breaking waves. The swell is considerable. The *Steve Irwin* is rolling slowly from side to side. The crew on the bridge are standing with their legs wide apart to keep their balance. But there's not a peep from anyone. Expressing reservations ahead of what could be our first confrontation is simply not done, especially not in the early stages of a campaign. I pull myself together, but the nerves remain.

The quartermasters and officers are staring to port, some with binoculars, others with their hands cupped above their eyes and pressed against the windows. The mist is hiding a monster that's slowly but surely creeping up on us.

Everybody on the bridge is expecting a vessel, but when a ship looms up out of the mist, it still comes as a surprise. 'Over there! Over there!' Jane yells. She jumps up and down and points to a dark shape, a couple of hundred yards from the *Steve Irwin*. 'I found it,' she cheers. 'I reckon it's a harpoon ship.'

As the ship sails closer, her outline appears. Peter Hammarstedt confirms Jane's suspicions: 'The high bow, the low gunwales and the high crow's nest. It's a harpoon ship, no doubt about it. The *Yushin Maru 2*, I think. We have to tell Paul.'

Peter uses the internal phone system to call the captain's cabin. A moment later, Captain Watson walks onto the bridge and takes the helm from the second mate. Most of the time the captain stays in his cabin, peering at charts, but as soon as there's a whiff of action, the bridge becomes his domain.

The harpoon on the bow is now clearly visible. Although the missile launcher is covered with a rain shield, the barrel is sticking out. The Japanese hunter comes within several dozen yards on port side before suddenly swerving to the left. It appears to be a reflex, suggesting that the Japanese crew have only just spotted our black pirate flag, which we quickly hoisted up our mast. A thick plume of black smoke shoots out of the *Yushin Maru*'s chimney. The Japanese are picking up speed, pointing their bow into the waves. They're getting away. With a top speed of 15 knots, the *Steve Irwin* is no match for the harpoon ships. Brilliantly designed, they are incredibly agile and can easily do up to 22 knots. Watson pursues the *Yushin* at full throttle, but he knows it's pointless unless we take other steps.

The wind is still raging fiercely. It may not be very sensible to deploy a dinghy, but nobody knows when we'll have another chance to tackle a harpoon ship. Launching it will be a gamble, and a risky one, but if this campaign were without danger, there'd be other vessels trying to stop these poachers at the edge of the world. And there aren't. It's up to this small band of volunteers. Without any form of consultation Watson announces: 'Launch the Delta.'

The captain opts for the lighter of the two rigid inflatable boats (RIBs) on board. In these weather conditions the Delta is easier to handle than the Gemini, which is nearly a tonne heavier. Normally I'm the navigator on the Gemini, but the deal is that when only the Delta is launched, I go along to throw butyric acid.

This foul-smelling, but otherwise innocent substance taints any whale meat that might be on board. Each minke whale Japan fails to sell is a financial setback for them. As well as physically obstructing the hunt, Sea Shepherd tries to expedite the whalers' bankruptcy. The butyric acid has the added advantage that the horrible stench makes working on deck impossible. As long as the whalers are sheltering in their cabins, we win.

Peter phones bosun Daniel Bebawi, who's out on deck, peering at the *Yushin Maru*. Team Delta is told to get ready for action. Daniel glances at the bridge, a worried look on his face, but immediately passes the message on to couple Andy and Molly. Andy is the Delta's helmsman, his fiancée its navigator. Meanwhile I pop by the media room and tell the ship's photographer that we're off.

He jumps up and grabs his cameras: the adrenaline junkie is up for a rough ride at sea.

The deckhands, or deckies as they're known aboard ship, gather on deck. Arne takes his place in front of the operating panel of the hydraulic crane. The blond German has been on board for months and has raised the tricky manoeuvres with the grab to an art form. A camera crew working for Animal Planet follows the deck team's every move. After the unexpected success of the reality TV series *Whale Wars*, the number of cameramen on the Sea Shepherd ship has tripled. One of the show's producers is stomping about angrily while yelling instructions at her crew. She has only just learnt that we're heading out, giving her not nearly enough time to prep a cameraman who will be joining us on board the inflatable.

While the deckies get the Delta ready, I have 10 minutes to launch. Time for a ritual dating back to my years with the police.

A night shift at the weekend usually meant scuffles, often with drunk idiots who could no longer tell a lamppost from a police officer. To psych myself up before my shift, I would always play two songs at home. As soon as the first few bars of Eminem's 'Lose Yourself' came blasting out of the stereo, I'd feel a jolt of excitement. Add to that Metallica's 'Enter Sandman' and I would arrive at the police station buzzing with adrenaline, all fired up to chase the bad guys. Since then I always listen to those tracks when things are about to kick off.

'You only get one shot, do not miss the chance to blow,' Eminem yells through my headphones. The chorus, which has become a mantra over the years, sounds more appropriate now than ever. Those bottles of butyric acid are supposed to land on the harpoon ship's deck. And I'll probably get just one chance. It all boils down to bringing out the best in myself. I have a job that everybody with Sea Shepherd dreams of: the action crew on the RIBs are the ultimate embodiment of the Antarctica campaign. The role is both the most satisfying and the most dangerous. The sea we love to protect is our greatest, most ruthless enemy. One mistake and the Antarctic waves swallow you up. If you're lucky, hypothermia sets in and you lose consciousness before you drown.

The thought of drowning scares me, but the final bars of Metallica usher me out on deck. We have to put the disaster scenarios out of our minds and perform our piece. The players are ready, the stage is a capricious blue-black sea, but what happens next is in the hands of the weather gods.

The icy polar wind welcomes every seaman stepping out onto the weather deck by sending a full-blown shiver through his body. The waves battering the *Steve Irwin*'s bow shoot a spray of seawater up into the air which, carried by the wind, splashes into our faces. The cold reality of Antarctica penetrates each and every pore.

On port side the harpoon ship is trying to escape. Arne, Simon and I are looking over the railing of the *Steve Irwin* at the Japanese. All three of us have our own reasons for hating the harpoon ship. Arne is a hardcore vegan who opposes animal cruelty in any shape or form. Simon is an eccentric biologist who believes that the planet's biodiversity must be preserved at all costs. And I'm here because I want to catch crooks. I think these whalers are criminals and we must do what we can to stop them. Decades ago, the international community banned commercial whaling and yet here is Japan, poaching the waters of a whale sanctuary. The Ministry of Fisheries is earning billions of yen from the extinction of a protected species. Somebody has got to stop these poachers. And if there's no action from any government bodies, then I guess it's up to a group of passionate amateurs to intervene. Every single crew member is prepared to put his or her life on the line. Our campaign feels like a last resort, the only way to save an endangered species.

A bucket full of bottles of butyric acid is loaded on to the Delta. Unfortunately the prop fouler is tied up on the Gemini. This thick, wire-wrapped mooring rope would be ideal in these circumstances. If the harpoon ship sails across the rope, the prop fouler will wrap itself around the propeller, forcing the whaler to stop for repairs. But we don't have enough time to put this secret weapon on board.

Arne operates the controls of the hydraulic crane with what looks like the greatest of ease. But his relaxed smile disappears the moment the grab tightens the steel cables and jolts the Delta out of its berth. With a thousand kilos dangling from the hook, it's now all down to precision and timing. If he misjudges the swell, the boat will end up swaying precariously above deck. The Delta must be lifted over the Gemini and onto the water. One slip-up and either the Delta's propellers or the top of the Gemini will be damaged.

Both the ship's company and the film crew are eyeing the crane operator's every move. The Sea Shepherd volunteers can't wait to chase the whalers, and the cameras are yearning for drama. A cameraman next to the crane machinist is alternately zooming in on his hands and face. Every single expression is caught on film. Arne ignores the cameras. He concentrates on the grab while following the bosun's instructions. Daniel glances over the railing to see if the first mate has reduced the speed to 8 knots. If we're going too fast, the *Steve Irwin*'s bow wave could cause the inflatable to capsize. He gives a thumbs-up to the bridge. Officer Peter does the same from the pilothouse: we're ready to launch.

When Daniel makes a flat-handed, sliding gesture towards starboard, Arne cranks the hydraulic arm across the Gemini. The wind tugs at the boat, but fails to get a hold on it. It sways a bit, that's all. With some nifty manoeuvring, Arne manages to place the Delta securely against the breasthook. Even the *Steve Irwin*'s rolling motion fails to dislodge it.

Andy and Molly step on board the Delta. Meanwhile Daniel frowns at the ocean and expresses his concerns quite openly, though out of Andy and Molly's earshot. 'The weather's getting worse. Look at those whitecaps. We must be up to force 5 by now.'

'It's not too bad,' says Peter, who's come out on deck to wish us luck. 'It could get better any minute and then it'll be calm for hours.'

It sounds promising, but our senses tell us otherwise: the sky is grey and we feel the tempestuous, biting wind in our faces. And besides: this is Antarctica, the South Pole, where the weather is always unpredictable.

Peter hugs everyone who's getting into the rubber boat. 'Good luck,' he adds, 'this is the moment we've all been working towards.' The remark fills me with pride. It's a welcome boost. My only RIB experience to date was in calm water and brilliant summer sunshine. All that's brilliant now are Peter's white teeth as he accompanies his encouraging words with a big smile. The rest of the world is grey and ominous.

A sign from Daniel and the crane machinist pulls the Delta away from our vessel. A mistake at this point could be fatal for the passengers. An accident is not an option, because in these waves a man overboard would disappear from sight within minutes, however bright his orange survival coverall.

As Arne eases the cables, the Delta jerks closer and closer to the water. The crew has to act quickly now. The second the rubber boat plunges into the water, Andy switches on the Delta's engine. Twin 90 horsepower roars above the howling wind. Molly tugs at the string of the snap hook so it comes off. Steel suspension cables crash onto the deck. Arne moves the grab away from the deckhands, who are clutching the bow and stern lines. They alone are keeping the Delta in place. The rubber boat bobs up and down on the water and is occasionally thrown against the ship's hull by a wave from behind. Andy and Molly are bouncing around the tiny boat like Duracell bunnies.

Deckhands open the heavy steel door on the side of the deck and unroll a rope ladder. The rest of the crew can go on board. First a cameraman, then the photographer. The latter clambers down with the cameras around his neck, jumps and lands on the Delta's inflated tube as if it's nothing. He quickly makes his way to a seat behind Molly and clings on while being pounded by the elements.

'What are you waiting for?' Captain Watson yells from the bridge wing. He scowls at Daniel, who's completely oblivious. 'The *Yushin*'s getting away. Come on, hurry up, launch that boat!' Daniel shakes his head. He seems to think this is insane, but keeps his mouth shut. And I don't blame him. Nobody says a word. Who'd be a coward? We'd rather die than be known as a quitter for the rest of the campaign should this first action be a success. That's peer pressure for you.

My turn. With each step towards the rope ladder that plunges down into the depths below, I feel more and more like a dead man walking. A deep breath. This is why I gave up my career as a police detective. This is what I've been dreaming of. Except that my vision showed a clear blue sky, a sea as smooth as a mirror and a heroic return to the ship, carrying a broken harpoon as a trophy. That's a distant memory now. One wrong move and I'll disappear between the hulls of the *Steve Irwin* and the Delta, lost in a swirling mass of water. Andy manoeuvres the Delta against the hull, but every wave pulls it away again. Barely a metre, but it feels like a monstrous, yawning gap. A foot that slips, a hand that misses, and I'll be dead. A victim. End of heroic epic.

With another deep gulp of air I climb down the ladder. Somewhere below me the Delta is rearing up like a rampant stallion. Standing on the bottom rung, I place one foot behind me on the tube. The other foot follows. Just as I'm about to turn, the Delta pulls away from the hull. My feet are dangling in the rubber boat, while my hands are desperately clinging on to the rope ladder. My body is a living suspension bridge between the Delta and the *Steve Irwin*. Andy immediately manoeuvres the boat back to the hull. 'Let go!' Molly yells anxiously. I don't think twice: I land in the Delta with a thump. Death lets me get away this time, but Andy doesn't let me reflect on it. He calmly tells me to untie the bowline. Still in a daze, I do as he says. Finally, the rubber boat is free from the *Steve Irwin*. We move away from the treacherous backwash as fast as we can.

On deck the other camera people become smaller and smaller. I bet they've captured the near-fatal incident in beautiful HD. On the bridge the captain is gesturing angrily. He points to port. We're steaming to starboard.

Andy doesn't notice the directions. He has to focus all his attention on steering as every single wave is out to capsize us. The radio is crackling. Somebody is trying to contact us, but we can't make out a voice. With this blustery wind whistling around our ears, we can barely even understand each other. Molly checks the GPS mounted on the dashboard and selects the waypoints which are supposed to lead us to the whaler. She points to the right. It makes no sense, but nobody knows why.

Meanwhile Andy is at risk of losing his battle with the ocean. Every time the Delta mounts and rides a wave, a free fall follows. The wind keeps trying to slip underneath the hull. At times it feels as if we're slamming vertically into the wind, so we lean forwards to prevent the boat from capsizing.

'The waves are far too high; we'll never pick up enough speed. And I can't see the *Steve* anymore...' Andy yells above the wailing wind. We're climbing higher and higher, and after each wave we plunge into a dark hole. We're caught in a funnel, closed in by walls of water. At our lowest all we can see are the crests. Andy keeps going while Molly tries to reset the GPS. After a surprise wave picks us up and dumps us several metres further on, Molly is flung against the console. Stunned and with a huge bump on her chin, she scrambles to her feet. She responds to my voice, but is visibly shaken. 'Go and sit behind Andy!' She follows my advice and I take over navigation duties.

By now the Delta has taken on a lot of water, and more is coming in with each surge. '*Steve Irwin*, *Steve Irwin*, this is the Delta, over,' I bark into the handheld radio. Crackling, followed by a male voice: we can't make sense of it. I try a couple more times. No answer.

'This is insane,' I shout to Andy. 'You're the skipper and you have the final say. It's up to you. This is beginning to look like a suicide mission. We can't see the *Yushin* or the *Steve* anywhere, Molly is injured and the weather is getting worse.'

Andy is in two minds. This is Operation Musashi's very first chase: nobody wants to fail. 'Try to get hold of the *Steve* one more time,' he says. 'Ask them for the *Yushin*'s position; perhaps they're still around.' No response from the *Steve Irwin*. 'Come on, what's it going to be? This is madness.' Andy is biding his time. On the crest of a wave I spot the dark-grey contours of the *Steve Irwin* on port. I point to it. 'Go back to the *Steve*, let's call it quits. The GPS is broken and we'll never catch up with the *Yushin*!' Andy nods, disappointed, but he too knows it's far too risky to keep going. Perhaps we should never have launched the Delta.

Closer to the *Steve Irwin* we finally manage to re-establish radio contact. The crew run out on deck and take up their positions. The photographer and me are the first to clamber up the rope ladder and get back on board. A cameraman from Animal Planet rushes over. He's met with a loud 'Fuck!' and I ignore the first couple of questions. Mixed feelings are the order of the day: anger because this action was stupid, and joy because we're still alive. Once the adrenaline has worn off, the interviewer is treated to a practised smile. Tough guys don't complain, especially not on TV.

As soon as Molly and Andy are back on deck in one piece, we're allowed to go and have a shower. Molly reports to the sickbay first. She has a big bruise and a mild concussion. A couple of days' rest and she'll be good to go back into the inflatable, according to the ship's doctor.

The battle has begun. Soon we'll track down the whaling fleet again, I know it. So what about the Delta's GPS? It was set to magnetic north, a setting that doesn't work in the Antarctic region. Beginner's error.

THE
MISSION

" *If you want to stop real pirates,*
you need other pirates to do it.
CAPTAIN PAUL WATSON "

01

DEATH WITHOUT WARNING

'HB 6301, HB 6301,' comes blaring out of the walkie-talkies sitting on the coffee table in front of us. The call doesn't register with us. Sebas is leaning back in his chair, feet on the table, rubbing the sleep from his eyes. I'm clutching a cup of coffee while staring dreamily out of the window, where the day, like me, is only slowly awakening.

'Hey, listen up,' yell the guys from the night shift we've just relieved. 'HB 6301, HB 6301,' the Haaglanden emergency control room repeats. This time, there's an edge to the woman's voice. She doesn't like to be kept waiting.

Sebas sits up straight: '6301, over.'

'6301, can you head over to Herenlaan in Maasland for a collision between a motorcyclist and a lorry, over?'

'Roger, five, over,' Sebas responds firmly.

'The ambulance is on its way and you've got clearance, 6301 over and out.'

Great: that means we get to go out there with all guns blazing. Sebas and I sprint to the patrol car and tear out of the yard with our sirens wailing. With a five on the walkie-talkie the control centre knows we're en route.

'That's got to be messy,' I say to my colleague while checking the glove compartment for a breathing mask.

'I suspect so. You're not likely to come out smiling after crashing your motorbike into a lorry. Do we need the GPS by the way?'

'No, you take the Coldenhove exit, then left at the roundabout and the first right.'

'Ah, that way.' Sebas manoeuvres our Mercedes at high speed left and right around the cars waiting at a red at the Westerlee junction. 'We'll be there in five,' he says as he puts his foot on the accelerator, doing close to 200 kilometres per hour.

'Let's stop by McD's for breakfast afterwards. I'm starving.'

Sebas takes the Coldenhove exit at top speed and races round the corner into Herenlaan. We press 'six' on the walkie-talkie: we've arrived at the scene. A couple of cars have come to a halt on the right side of the road. A motorcyclist is lying motionless in front of them, his seriously damaged motorbike a couple of metres away. Parked behind him is a semi-trailer without a lorry. With the breathing equipment in my hand, I rush over to the victim. Sebas runs over to the driver of the front car, whose eyes are darting around all over the place and who's pacing back and forth with a mobile phone glued to his ear.

The motorcyclist is lying on the tarmac in an unnatural position. His legs are crumpled beside him and bumps are visible under his leather trousers, hinting at several broken bones. His face is unrecognisable; a pulp of bloody flesh, bone and brains swimming around in his crash helmet. Dark red blood seeps out from under his visor and leaves a growing, jagged stain on the road.

The victim's arm lies limp in my hand. My fingers are trying to find a pulse on the inside of his wrist. For a couple of seconds, the blood throbs in his veins, but the pauses between the beats are lengthening. During those pauses I'm completely oblivious to the world around me. All I do is listen to the pounding of his heart until it stops. CPR is pointless as his chest is shattered and his face gone. Damn, what's keeping that ambulance? They're the specialists. Maybe they can save him. Vain hope, I know, but I'd rather hope in vain than give up. Sebas comes and stands beside me. 'And?'

'Can you check? I can't feel a pulse anymore.' My colleague crouches down and repeats what I just did.

'No, I don't feel anything either.' He gets up and quietly looks at the young guy on the ground for a moment.

'What's keeping that fucking ambulance?'

'No idea, it should be here soon. The control room said they were on their way. The victim works over there, by the way.' Sebas points to a large white building housing a fruit and vegetable wholesaler, a few hundred metres up the road. 'How bizarre is that?'

'How do you know?'

'His colleagues are all in these cars here.'

'Jesus, keep them away, will you, because this is looking nasty.'

Sebas walks back to the main witness, who's still pacing up and down in front of his car, looking shell-shocked.

A little later the ambulance finally arrives. The medics make a last-ditch attempt to save the young man, but they too conclude that the motorcyclist has died. There's nothing they can do. Meanwhile, more onlookers have gathered, all wanting to know how their colleague is doing. The answer is painfully clear when the ambulance staff cover the body with a white sheet.

I can't think straight for the cloud of gloom that's hanging over me. The only thing going through my mind is that I'm 21 and have just seen a man die. My knees are shaking and I'm half-expecting my legs to give way under me. One of the medics grabs me by the shoulder. 'Are you OK?' I nod, but a big lump settles in my stomach. There's only one way I can stop myself from lingering on what has just happened and that's to focus on the job expected of a police officer: establish the facts and make sure the investigation goes off without a hitch.

The control room calls up an inspector from the Naaldwijk station to coordinate the investigation. Colleagues are on their way to direct the traffic. A little later the accident scene is awash with police, all looking for an answer to the question: who is to blame for this accident? Was the driver allowed to park his trailer on this suburban road? Was the motorcyclist going too fast?

The inspector rolls the body onto its side and pulls out a wallet from the motorcyclist's pocket. Although the bystanders have given us a good idea of the guy's identity, we have to be sure. His driving licence gives us the information we need. 'Marc van Rosenburg,' the investigating officer informs us. 'Born 17 September 1976.' Four years older than me. And now he's dead. He went to work as usual this morning. He showered, brushed his teeth, prepared some sandwiches and probably kissed his girlfriend goodbye before he got on his motorbike. On his way to work his mind may have wandered to an upcoming holiday, or perhaps to the purchase of a great new motorbike. Dreams that have come to an abrupt end because of a trailer on Herenlaan, a hundred metres from his workplace.

Now that the victim's identity is known, two officers are dispatched to his parents' home. They leave with a heavy heart. I'm glad it's not me. It's not a popular task within the force. Police officers want to catch crooks. What they don't want is to deliver sad news to two unsuspecting parents who are just starting their day.

Once the remains have been taken to the mortuary, and the forensics team has finished collecting evidence, the fire brigade arrives at the scene to sweep up the remaining debris and hose down the road. If it weren't for some chalk marks, which will fade in due course, it would look as if nothing had ever happened here. Cars are beginning to pass again, slowly making their way to the business up the road. My first-ever fatal incident has been wrapped up.

Without a word, we drive back to the station, passing the weeping willows in the verge, silent witnesses to a horrible accident.

It's eerily quiet in the patrol car on the way back. Sebas is shaken too. I don't know what to say, or think. Besides, what is there to think: someone has died and for everybody except his family, friends and colleagues the world will keep turning. Just before we get to the station I say to Sebas: 'Why don't we skip McD's?' He bursts out laughing. Wry humour helps us cope.

At the station, colleagues are at the ready to support us. Most of them have experience of fatal accidents and are familiar with the feelings we're grappling with. Our boss tells us that we have to go and see someone at employee support and counselling. 'We're going for a smoke first,' we reply in unison and make our way to the garage, the only place where you're allowed to light up these days.

A sergeant of about 50, clearly bored, is plucking some tobacco from a pouch. His yellow fingers roll another cigarette. He joined this station as a trainee. His faded blue uniform hangs unironed on his body. He owes his rank to his mentoring role, rather than any sort of competence. There was really no more room for someone who'd been cutting corners for years, but, as the chief inspector said trying to justify his decision, this would enable him to pass his knowledge on to new recruits.

'In my day...' the sergeant begins, before licking the paper and lighting his roll-up. Sebas and I look at one another: we're in for a tall tale from the old days, which is just about the last thing we need. 'Whenever we had a stiff, we'd buy a round. There was no such thing as employee support. You just did what you had to do; it toughened you up. Back then the bodies were taken to the mortuary in the basement of the police station, but now they give you psychiatric support at the drop of a hat. What rubbish!'

These are the words of a man grown bitter by everything his policeman's eyes had seen and his memory had repressed. The sergeant never had the guts to talk about his traumas or to swap his dead-end job for something new. Now that it's too late, there's nothing this frustrated man can do but pass his days glued to a folding chair in the smoking area. Behind a gaze that was once tough and hard as nails are eyes begging for attention that will never come. His comments make me realise that I don't ever want to become this jaded. I stub out my cigarette and go and see employee support. Reluctantly, but anything is better than ending up like this miserable blue heap with trembling yellow fingers.

'How do you feel?' the counsellor asks perfunctorily.

'Um well, weird… and kind of shit.'

'How come?' is the second obvious question, which strikes me as a bit insensitive. I talk about the accident, what I felt and what I did. Although I didn't fancy having this conversation, sharing my experience comes as a relief. Thirty minutes later I'm out. I'm going to smoke a cigarette. And then another one.

After that tragic day, the fatal accident haunts me for weeks. It's not that I wake up screaming, but I'm preoccupied with the meaning of this fragile life. All I can think of are the various answers to the question: what would I do if I knew my life was going to end soon?

Several months later the forensics department concludes that the trailer had been parked correctly. The owner explained that he had put the trailer temporarily under a lamppost so it would be more clearly visible. What he failed to realise was that right underneath the light source the trailer was actually less noticeable. The motorcyclist had probably been riding with his dark visor down – perhaps to avoid the glare from the rising sun. In the dawn light he failed to notice the trailer. Travelling at about 50 kilometres per hour, he crashed into it. Nobody was punishable and the public prosecutor decided not to take action. Case closed.

Bad luck would have been a valid conclusion too. Bad luck, and a healthy young man is ripped from this life. That conclusion kept haunting me. An ordinary day is brutally disrupted just because two people make a perfectly innocent mistake.

During my years with the force many more dead would follow. Manslaughter, murder and suicide – of both strangers and colleagues. But above all: road deaths. Tragedies I could never get my head round; the unfairness of a fatal accident, the arbitrariness: one minute you're on your way somewhere, the next you're breathing your last. It was beyond my comprehension. And someone who doesn't understand things gets angry. With death, because it cuts short healthy people's lives without warning. And with life, because it allows this terrible, unpredictable business without putting up a fight.

At the end of the day I had two options: I could allow the powerlessness to build into unresolved traumas and turn into a psychological wreck, or I could view every horrible experience as the most valuable lesson of my time with the force. A lesson that teaches you that every day is precious and you should make the most of it. I opted for the latter and decided that the motorcyclist hadn't died completely in vain.

02

PIECES OF THE PUZZLE

Slowly, agonisingly slowly, Maarten pulls the elastic band off his lunch box. And just as leisurely he lifts the lid to reveal his lunch. No surprise there: the cheese and tomato sandwiches are the detective's daily fare. Tucked in beside the slices of brown bread are an apple and a twin-pack of biscuits. The apple will be consumed during our walk after lunch, the two biscuits during the three o'clock coffee break. He bites into one of the sandwiches and chomps and chews in a rhythm I've previously observed in camels, calmly ruminating in a desert oasis somewhere.

But Maarten is sitting under the white striplighting in the canteen at the Ridderkerk police station. Other colleagues are visibly annoyed by his sluggishness. Everybody wants to get out and spend the remaining 16 minutes of our lunch break in the fresh air. But Maarten, completely oblivious, munches on until the second sandwich, too, has disappeared. Occasionally he holds forth about bygone days in which a tough young Maarten rode around town without a helmet, provoking the authorities and making eyes at pretty girls. But stare as I might at his lanky body, dull eyes and grey hair, I can't reconcile the two images.

Maarten's life, so utterly devoid of joie de vivre, makes me feel sick. At least that's what I thought, but the more I feel the loathing, the more I realise it's directed at myself. Nothing remains of the promise I made a couple of years ago: to make the most out of life. Look what's become of me: a detective with the Interregional Environmental Crime Team of the Rotterdam-Rijnmond force, labouring over hopeless cases with colleagues whose passion for the job didn't survive their training.

During my stint as a bobby on the beat, I knew I wanted to be a detective. Not a detective constable who interrogates junkies and shoplifters, but a proper one, the kind who exposes organised crime. Preferably environmental crime, because nature conservation was more important to me than cocaine busts.

To convince my superiors of my investigative skills I had to have more to show for myself than experience and heaps of enthusiasm. An undergraduate foundation course would do the trick, I reckoned.

In my spare time I embarked on a part-time journalism course and after completing the first year, I showed my certificate to the head of the environmental team. But I enjoyed the writing so much that I decided to study for a couple more years. During that time I did a work placement with the Goudsche Courant newspaper, and that's where I first noticed 'lunch box syndrome'. At 12 o'clock sharp, the workers would trot off to the canteen, like cattle to their troughs. And these were newspaper journalists I'd always put on a pedestal: men and women spending all day sniffing out the latest scoops and bashing away at their keyboards until a world-changing article reached the editorial desk just before the morning paper went to print. In reality they were a little less driven. Conscientiously, the workers would eat their homemade sandwiches in a sparsely furnished canteen. Within 30 minutes, or the boss would get annoyed. In fact, after 20 minutes they would nervously push their chairs back to make way for the 12.30 shift. Journalists in a straitjacket: no free spirits with a passion for all things news-related, but part of the office furniture and with a guaranteed pension. I wasn't going to let that happen to me.

But in spite of my best intentions I found myself in a similar situation on the Environmental Team. Whereas I'd envisaged tracking down networks of international poachers, the work of a cross-regional environmental detective wasn't quite what I had expected. It took three investigations for this to dawn on me.

The first was a case involving illegal fireworks. Piles of firecrackers confiscated, a couple of Chinese suspects sentenced and excellent publicity for the Rotterdam police force. And yet the investigation gave me little satisfaction. After all, those bangers could be purchased legally just across the Belgian border.

This was followed by a criminal investigation into illegal sludge dumping. Well, I say illegal, but sometimes processed factory sewage may be spread on land, sometimes not. The public prosecutor cited minutiae from convoluted environmental and soil protection laws to build up a case. Months of painstaking work resulted in minimal penalties. And so-called legal sewage sludge is still being dumped on Dutch agricultural land. Whether or not it makes your potatoes grow crooked or come out orange doesn't seem to matter, as long as the laws are complied with. I didn't get it then and I still don't get it now.

Finally, we took on a case that made my green heart beat faster: the illegal trade in endangered birds of prey. At various locations throughout the Netherlands, shady characters were dealing in flying predators, ranging from buzzards to extremely rare black eagles and, in one case, even an Andean Condor. A suspect in Zuid-Holland was selling a lot of these beautiful creatures. During a raid on his business, we found hundreds of birds of prey confined to cages made of wood and mesh and no bigger than a couple of square metres.

And guess what? Again, no laws had been breached. It turned out that endangered animal species are legal commodities as long as the trade regulations in the Convention on International Trade in Endangered Species (CITES) treaty are complied with. And it's easy to obtain the right paperwork in the corrupt countries where most of these birds are disappearing from the wild.

After seeing these magnificent birds in those hideous cages and knowing that another miscarriage of justice was imminent, a fire ignited in me. This was wrong. We had the means to take action, but what with corruption and red tape it was business as usual for these poachers. The police couldn't stop these criminals, so something else needed to be done. A profound urge to liberate these rare creatures from their wretched cages was beginning to muscle in on my duty to keep within the letter of the law.

While the investigation continued for many more months, I became less and less interested in enforcing the law. Environmental activists began to catch my attention. Because I'd been a vegetarian for years I was familiar with books such as *Animal Liberation* and other animal rights literature. Now that the fire had been stoked, more radical books followed, including *The Monkey Wrench Gang*, *Free the Animals* and *Empty Cages*. I took refuge in texts about the liberation of maltreated animals, but reading wasn't enough. Before long I was joining demonstrations against animal cruelty. The wearing of leather and fur, the consumption of meat and fish, animal testing: suddenly, it was all objectionable to me. But alas, shouting in the street offered no solace. The more demos I attended, the less I believed that this congregation of ripped jeans, tatty dreadlocks, hippie dresses and angry faces would ever achieve anything.

Now what? The environmental police gave me no satisfaction, nor did the groups of protesting activists. An exploration of various environmental organisations followed. World Wildlife Fund? Too cuddly. The Party for the Animals? Political hogwash. How about Greenpeace? Too much protest. And smaller grassroots organisations didn't appeal to me. Nothing gave me a warm feeling. Until I clicked on a YouTube video while surfing the web. The visual quality was poor, as it was probably cut by an enthusiast in some attic, but while playing 'This Is Sea Shepherd' I heard Captain Paul Watson uttering these magic words:

'We spend billions of dollars searching through the solar system for intelligent life to communicate with when we have intelligent life right here on our planet with us that we don't even attempt to talk to or communicate with. Intelligence is the ability to live in harmony with your natural world. By that criteria, we're the stupidest of species.

'We will lose more species of plants and animals between 1980 and 2045 than we have lost in the past 65 million years. That rate of extinction is unprecedented and we, as one species, are responsible for that.

'The oceans are dying in our time. And if the navies in this world had any kind of responsibility, they would be protecting the oceans instead of playing silly little war games with each other.

'The problem is that we have all the rules, the regulations and the treaties we need to protect the world's oceans and marine wildlife in them, but we don't have any enforcement… There are no fishermen anymore. There are corporations that are destroying the oceans…

'I know it's a little chilly here today, but we recently just came back from a place that's a little cooler than this and that's Antarctica. My crew and I just returned from chasing the Japanese whaling fleet along the coast of Antarctica. We chased them for 4,000 sea miles, for 50 days.

'Piracy was shut down in the Caribbean by Henry Morgan, a pirate. If you want to stop real pirates, you need other pirates to do it. So we're pirates of compassion, but we're hunting down and destroying pirates of profit…

'The fleet just returned to Japan and they were 85 whales short of their quota. So we were able to protect 85 whales.

'This is a growing movement. It's the most important movement in the world. That is the movement of saving life, of saving the earth. It means that we have to stand up and say: "Look, we're going to take matters into our hands, as individuals, as caring, compassionate people. And we're going to fight back, because the one thing that is worth fighting for on this planet Earth is life."'

Something clicked. For several minutes, I stared at the screen. Stunned. Dolphins, whales, sea turtles, my childhood spent on the Westland coast, the brown, muddy water of the North Sea, eating herring near Hook of Holland, granddad's delicious smoked mackerel, fish suffocating in overflowing nets, plastic bags floating in the oceans: beautiful and sad associations with the sea flashed before my eyes.

I pressed 'play' a second time. Once again I heard Paul Watson's voice. His words are accompanied by images of men and women in rubber boats chasing harpoon ships. The clip shows whalers cutting dead whales to ribbons. Whales that are protected under international treaties, that are swimming in a sanctuary. Until I saw these images, I thought whaling was a thing of the past, of the previous century, banned in the 1980s. But it turns out that Japan harpoons them in their masses. And aside from some half-hearted political pressure, nobody is doing anything except Sea Shepherd, or so the video claimed.

My head was spinning. My body tingling with excitement. Would I have the guts to join that boat? After my umpteenth viewing of the clip, I visited the conservation society's website.

Sea Shepherd was looking for volunteers to embark on its ship, the M/Y *Steve Irwin*. According to the mission statement, they're engaged in a worldwide hunt for poachers. They're trying to stop criminals where nobody else is. The organisation draws on the United Nations' World Charter for Nature to justify its actions. The manifesto provides authority to both individuals and organisations to help protect endangered wildlife species.

Photos of previous campaigns showed actions against whaling and the Canadian seal hunt. In Japan two volunteers actually jumped into the water near Taiji to free captured dolphins from the nets. I knew enough: these were heroes, modern resistance fighters protecting marine wildlife without violence against people. Heroic action on the high seas, little appreciation for what they do, minimal means and volunteers far outnumbered by the poachers. This was a David versus Goliath scenario – the romance of adventure leapt off my computer screen.

With the prospect of hunting down poachers, a great adventure and the conservation of the planet, all the pieces of the puzzle fell into place: I had found a purpose.

03

THE LAST DROP

The barman at my local, De Oude Jan in Delft, puts two pints in front of us. They go down very well in the early spring weather. It's just what I need. Despite the awe-inspiring introduction to Sea Shepherd, I still haven't taken any steps to get on board and it's really pissing me off.

'All those self-help books help fuck all,' I say to my best friend Richard. 'Make the most of what you've got... Yeah, whatever. But it doesn't stop you from trying to find the meaning of life.'

'Exactly,' Richard says without looking at me. He's distracted by a cute little skirt bravely catching the first few rays of sunshine.

'The police are a good employer, but I feel like a puppet, a number following orders. I'm sure there are hundreds of detectives who love this job, but I'm not one of them.'

My mate sips his lager, but doesn't say anything. I feel like I'm talking to myself. We watch the skirt disappear behind the bridge across the canal.

'It's not satisfying enough. It's adventure I'm after. Right now, the only excitement in my life is the early morning choice between traffic jam and public transport.'

'That's sad all right,' says Richard, who's fed up with my moaning. He signals to the barman, who serves us two more pints.

'What is it you really want to do?'

'Join that boat.'

'The Sea Shepherd one?'

'Yup, those guys are doing great work. I spent some time volunteering – translating and leafleting at festivals and the like. And I've met a couple of people who've been on board. Their stories make me want to join.'

'You know,' my best friend sounds irritable, 'maybe you should stop bullshitting and actually do something. Piss off abroad, risk it. You can always come back if it all goes pear-shaped.' If only it were that easy. A well-paid job, a house, a car, family in the Netherlands and a lovely Australian girlfriend: all certainties that stop me from taking the plunge. The contents of my beer glass disappear down my throat.

'Yeah, but...' I fall silent. There's always the 'yeah, but'. The 'but' that is followed by 'my job, my degree, my family, my finances'. The strangulating 'but' that strikes a death blow to every promising plan.

We change the subject. Aided by copious amounts of alcohol, we reminisce about dodgy holiday adventures and fantasise about changing the world. We drink to the past and the future, while we drown the present right here and now in the pub.

'That's enough,' announces the throbbing headache that inevitably follows hours of drinking in the sun. Richard staggers over to the train station, while I head home, lurching through the Prinsenhof. In the public garden, in front of the statue of William of Orange, I empty my full bladder in the bushes. Two blurred outlines of the father of the nation appear to be frowning at my splattering offence. The man who drove out the Spaniards is a hero, a war hero no less. I like heroes. People who escape the patronising opinions of others, who do what needs doing and become sources of inspiration in the process. William must have thought something along these lines. Must have wanted to distinguish himself or prove to himself that he was brave enough to take risks. But who cares about the motivation? Here he is, cast in bronze. I button up my trousers and stagger away from William. After a couple of steps I've all but forgotten our national hero.

The alcohol slowly lulls me to sleep, but before I drift off to dreamland where I'm a bona fide hero, I go through the promises we all make while drunk and on the brink of sleep. Tomorrow I'll start dieting, tomorrow I'll stop smoking, tomorrow I'll better my life, tomorrow everything will be different. But tomorrow nothing will be different. My tomorrow is always the same, day in day out.

Tomorrow I'll really start making the most of my life, I promise the motorcyclist who reminds me of my good intentions just before I fall asleep. Tomorrow I'll no longer be that jaded environmental detective who's stuck in traffic in the morning and who has a 15-minute coffee break at 10. Tomorrow I'll no longer sleepwalk through life. Whether or not I fell asleep with a blissful smile on my face that night, I don't know, but the next morning I woke up remembering the previous night's promises. This time it was for real.

04

FAREWELL

'Mum, Dad: I'm emigrating to Australia.' Both knew I'd been thinking about it for some time, but now that I've made up my mind, there's an awkward silence. My father stops eating his meatballs, my mother looks away, trying to fight back tears.

'I'm moving in with my girlfriend, but eventually I want to join the Sea Shepherd boat.'

'What about your job?' my father asks, surprised.

'I've handed in my notice.'

'What?!' He glares at me: my travels plans have got through to him. 'You're throwing away your career with the force because you want to join those ecoterrorists? Some stray hippies on a boat? In God's name, why? Why can't you just take a couple of weeks off, like any other normal human being?'

No, I think. There can be no half measures. I have to give it my all and say goodbye to everything at home, or it won't happen.

'Because I want to follow my dreams and stop the whalers.'

'You're out of your mind! You were doing so well with the police. A detective at such a young age. You could have become a commissioner, for God's sake.'

There's no point trying to explain my motivation when the ingredients of a good life are thought to be work, home and children. Meanwhile my mother is muttering that she'll never see me again. We've got Skype, I reassure her, but my words fall on deaf ears. The minute I get on that plane, I'll be lost forever. I can't convince her otherwise.

'What about your journalism degree?' my father asks.

'I'm chucking it in. After two years I reckon I know how to write. I don't think I need to finish the degree.'

My parents sit there staring at me; they just don't get it.

'You're completely insane.' My father means it from the bottom of his heart.

'What about your debts?' he resumes, reminding me of things that might make me change my mind.

'I've got enough money to make the repayments for at least a year. We'll see after that.'

'You're shirking your responsibilities. You shouldn't be running from your commitments here.'

'And stay in this country for the next 20 years to pay it all back? No way. I'll be earning lots of money one day and then I'll pay it back.'

'Who are you kidding?'

'I'm serious.'

But the truth is that I've run up a debt of 15,000€ to finance my degree and a car. I can only pay off the interest on my loan for about two months. At most. Then I'll be in trouble, but no way am I going to admit this to my parents.

'You're acting like a teenager. You have no idea what you're doing. You've well and truly lost your mind.'

My father launches into a tirade. His surprise has turned into impotent rage: this is the last-ditch rescue effort of a desperate parent who knows that his child is slipping away from him. It doesn't make the slightest bit of difference.

The surprise and anger are followed by acquiescence. A pause for us to catch our breath after the storm of recriminations. My father chews a meatball, while my mum, who doesn't quite know what to do with herself, starts clearing the table before I've even started eating my veggie burger.

'We'll drop you off at the airport,' I hear my mother blubbing from the kitchen. With tears pouring down her cheeks, she returns to the table with three bowls of custard. 'It's your choice. I know we can't talk you out of it. If this is what you want, then so be it. We don't want you to go, but your father and I will always love you.' My father nods in agreement with my mum's kind words. I hate to see them unhappy.

Now that my family has been informed, I start preparing openly. First up, my rental flat in Delft: I give notice the next day. The landlord already has a new tenant in mind, a young guy who'll be living on his own for the first time. Since I need to get rid of my furniture and things, I've asked him to drop by one Saturday afternoon. It's a simple choice: spend weeks messing about on eBay to get a couple more euros, or spare myself the time and trouble and offer the whole shebang to the new tenant. No sooner has he entered the house than I launch into my sales pitch.

'There's a nearly new washing machine. Most of the appliances in the kitchen are new. The sofa belonged to the previous occupant; everything else is IKEA. It's all yours for 2,000€.' The new tenant must think there's a catch. These items are worth at least twice as much. I tell him that I'm emigrating and can't be bothered to haggle. 'I suspect you'll have to ditch the sofa, it's full of holes. And it's been gnawed at by the rats.'

'Rats?'

'I had two pet rats, Plato and Socrates. They used to run around freely in the living room and would nibble at the odd thing.' Only a minute ago he was introduced to a police officer, but now he thinks I'm a weirdo. I can tell by the look in his eyes.

'1,500.'

'Deal.'

I spend the remaining couple of weeks at my parents' house in De Lier. I've sold my car, booked my flight, had my name removed from the municipal register, cancelled all my insurance policies and subscriptions and organised a farewell party at the local tennis club. What stays with me most about the terrific send-off are the bets made behind my back about the length of my stay in Australia. Three days according to the greatest pessimist – who may or may not have been my brother – while the highest bid was three months. Not exactly morale boosting. My new life on the other side of the globe clearly doesn't inspire a lot of confidence. My father isn't alone in thinking that I don't follow things through. Save for a handful of people, it's the general consensus.

With my departure imminent, parting is becoming a painful reality. My life is in a backpack in the boot of the car. Clothes and a laptop, that's all I'm taking Down Under. Knowing that I have no more possessions gives me an indescribable sense of freedom. A man who owns nothing can go anywhere in life.

The argument is wasted on my mother, who's no longer fighting her tears. She cries throughout our drive to the train station in Delft. The rest of the family is absent. My brother and sister are at work, my father has commitments abroad. Having been months in the pipeline, my departure is no longer anything special. Besides, they all think I'll be back soon.

My mother and I don't talk much while we're waiting for the train to Schiphol Airport. There are no words for that moment when two people think differently but feel the same.

'We'll miss you. Take good care of yourself.'

'I'll miss you too, Mum, badly. But I have to do this.'

'I know, but I don't understand.' Her last few words drown in a flood of tears.

Luckily my train arrives, so I can hide my distress behind the sliding doors and leave my mother upset, but waving, on the platform.

Check-in, passport control, security: it all passes in a blur. I think about everything I'm leaving behind: my family, friends, the tennis club and my house. I'm having second thoughts. Am I making the right choice? Will it all work out? Who can I fall back on? I have to make a success of it. But what if it doesn't work out, what if I fail? As the plane taxies to the runway, I'm torn between fear and excitement. But the minute we take off, I simply let go. There's no way back now: my new life has begun.

05

FREEING CHICKENS

Even from a distance, the 'black legend' is quite conspicuous among the grey vessels. Impressed, I make my way from Flinders Street Station to the Melbourne Docklands, where the Sea Shepherd flagship is moored. In the 1970s this robust Scottish patrol vessel ploughed through the stormy waters of the North Sea, now it's biding its time in Australia until, in early December, it gets to go back to hunting the Japanese whalers in the Antarctic. The closer I come, the more I want a place on board the M/Y *Steve Irwin*.

In front of the ship, a volunteer is handing out leaflets to curious passers-by. Other young people dressed in black T-shirts with the logo 'Sea Shepherd Crew' are walking up and down the gangplank, lugging boxes filled with fruit, vegetables and other supplies. At the top, they turn on their heels and come back down with full bin bags that disappear in the refuse containers on the quayside.

When I ask her where to find the crew coordinator, the volunteer kindly tells me that it's Chris Aultman. As well as the helicopter pilot, he's also the one responsible for selecting the crew. Would I mind looking for him myself?

A little nervous, I cross the gangplank and go on deck, which is permeated by a powerful smell of crystallised seawater and steel. Inside, the deceptively small-looking vessel is a maze of corridors and narrow staircases. After finding myself at a dead end three times, I finally arrive in the dining area, where some visitors are watching a promotional video on a gigantic television donated by supporters. Seated at the long dining table, Daniel Bebawi is devouring his lunch. Nearby, in the galley, a couple of women are juggling with hot pans. I'd better not get in their way. Daniel explains obligingly that Chris is probably on the helicopter deck, up two flights of stairs and then straight ahead.

'The ship's full.' Wearing green pilot coveralls and a goofy cap, the crew coordinator shatters my long cherished desire with one short sentence. Looking at me from behind his round spectacles he's trying to be sympathetic. 'Maybe you can come along at the end of January, early February, when we return to refuel for the second leg. Have you sent in your application?' Chris becomes overly friendly when he realises that the man he's talking to has been reduced to a series of disjointed vowels.

'Uh, yes, back in the Netherlands. I'll try again when you guys come back, thanks and good luck with Operation Migaloo.' With my tail between my legs, I slink off from the *Steve Irwin*.

Back on shore, the information girl asks me to help carry some boxes with donations that have just been dropped off. Together with some burly volunteers, we lug the cardboard boxes on deck, where they're passed through a hatch and stored in the freezer.

The solidarity and friendliness of the Sea Shepherd volunteers: I'd love to be a part of this. I decide to put my best foot forward and to try again at the end of January. I do odd jobs until dusk and head home after a free vegan meal. In the days that follow I do as much as I can to help ready the vessel for its campaign. But not every day, because now that my trip to sea is off I need to earn money to pay my rent.

My new life as an Australian worker is spent sticking labels on clothes in a garment warehouse for a couple of dollars per hour. A job my girlfriend has fixed up for me. In my mind's eye I'm standing on the bow of the *Steve Irwin*, with the wind in my hair. In reality, I'm standing at a conveyor belt in a musty depot, poorly paid and surrounded by immigrant workers who don't speak a word of English, let alone Dutch. Only a few weeks in and my Australian dream appears to be showing some cracks.

But not for long. In my spare time, I take up Wing Chun kung fu again. Melbourne boasts the biggest school specialising in this martial art, and it's where the great Chinese master himself teaches his best students. It's been several years since my last lesson, but it only takes a couple of sessions for my rusty limbs to get back into the swing of things. This doesn't go unnoticed by a Dutch instructor who's in town for a teaching stint. Before I know it, he offers me an admin job. In exchange I get to train full-time and receive expenses. It's a deal. Anything is better than sorting the latest fashions at six in the morning.

To build up a social life I volunteer for animal rights organisation Animal Liberation Victoria. The people I meet there become good friends. Despite my police background they invite me to help out at demos and actions, usually behind the scenes. This continues until the end of December.

'How would you like to come along to an open rescue?' founder Patty Mark asks me. 'Great.' An open rescue is another term for breaking into a chicken shed, a pig farm or any other place where animals are kept under appalling conditions. Damage to buildings is kept to a minimum, the diseased animals are rescued and the whole thing is filmed openly. Several months later the ALV returns to film the enormous differences between the diseased chickens, who have since recovered their health, and the chickens still living in the shed.

These images are then disseminated online. Needless to say, the location is kept a strict secret. On 31 December, with Australia about to uncork the champagne, we set off to liberate chickens.

Our driver is drumming his fingers on the wheel, nervous and impatient to leave the crowded city, which is crawling with police on New Year's Eve. We load our tools and drive out of Melbourne just before midnight.

The chicken shed is about a 90-minute drive away. We're about to liberate broiler breeder chickens – fowl that grow fast and only produce chicks for their meat. Thousands and thousands of these breeder chickens are packed tight in gigantic sheds, where they're largely neglected because all they're supposed to do is lay eggs and hatch them. After they finish laying eggs, they're usually sold off as boiling hens.

It's pitch-dark when our driver stops by the side of the road. On his signal, we leap out of the car and hide in the tall grass on the verge. The minivan drives off, while we wait, pressed close to the cold ground, for the green light. The crescent moon remains largely hidden behind passing clouds. The darker the better, because nobody must see us here. Luckily there's no street lighting in these rural parts. Nor do I spot a single house with the lights on. Noah, our leader, whispers that we're moving on. We follow him in pairs until he halts in front of an enormous shed. He points to it. Here goes. The adrenaline surges through my body: less than six months ago, I might have arrested these burglars after an emergency call. Now I'm one of them.

'Duck...' Noah meant to whisper, but he's so tense his voice cracks. We all jump behind the trees on the verge. In the silence the team's jagged breathing is deafening. There's a lot at stake for all of us. Arrest means a criminal record. In the worst case, people will lose their jobs. I'll be chucked out of the country – the authorities will immediately revoke my visa. And yet I didn't think twice. First of all because I think rescuing these chickens is a good thing, and second because I want to prove to myself that I'm an activist.

In the distance two headlights can be seen inching up the road towards our country lane. If they turn into it, they'll spot our driver. In these parts, an unfamiliar vehicle usually suggests there's something amiss. It's not unusual for farmers here to carry a weapon. Patty failed to mention this. According to her, almost all actions pass off without a hitch. Almost. So does this one, because the car passes.

We all heave a sigh of relief. The novices are looking a little green around the gills. Noah laughs: to him the open rescues are child's play. He sprints across the road and the rest follow. The activist clambers over the fence and fiddles with the padlock: it's not actually locked. We slip through, quick as a flash.

We switch our headlamps on. The dim light casts an eerie glow over the old dark shed. Work clothing hangs on the wall, with boots underneath it, and right next to it a white china washbasin that has seen better days. Each step kicks dust and sawdust off the concrete floor. The stale air immediately hits your lungs. The place looks as if no one's been here for days.

Patty hands out disposable white coveralls which we put on over our clothes. We're also given a surgical mask, because the air in this place can't be healthy. When we walk over to the chickens, we're met by a pungent odour of urine, faeces and rotting meat.

As far as our torches reach, we can see fluffy hens running around the darkened shed. The fowl tumble over one another as they try to keep out of our way. After a couple of minutes, they calm down a bit and a little later the first few chickens are scratching in the sawdust again. It's hard not to tread on them, because the shed is chock-a-block. Many of the young chicks have minor injuries caused by their own kind. 'They're so stressed they pull out their own and other chickens' feathers,' one of the activists explains. 'And they're constantly pecking at each other,' she continues while separating a fighting pair.

A sad-looking Patty picks up dead, rotting chickens scattered here and there among the scratching fowl and puts them in a bin bag. 'No wonder there's bird flu,' she says angrily.

These chickens are so overfed that some collapse under their own weight. Here and there, a chick without the use of its legs flaps its wings and drags itself a couple of inches across the floor. Others are motionless, waiting to be attacked or to die of dehydration.

While the inexperienced activists give the chickens food and water, Noah and Patty select the fowl that are in greatest need and may still be saved. They pick 12 that will come with us. Their frightened little heads poke out of the bags, unaware that among these many thousands they're the lucky ones escaping this poultry hell.

We leave the other fowl with full troughs and fresh drinking water. We exit the dark barn in low spirits, because we really want to rescue them all. No creature deserves such terrible suffering.

Noah waits by the side of the road for our driver's headlights. They're approaching rapidly from behind the hill. He double-checks to see if they do indeed belong to our minivan. The driver signals with full beam. We climb over the fence and hand over the cackling chickens as fast as we can. Then we roll headlong into the minivan and slam the sliding doors shut. Our vehicle tears down the country lane. Nobody says a word; we're not safe yet. Patty puts the chickens into crates. The little critters burble softly to themselves.

Once we're a safe distance away, our tense faces break into broad, out-and-out smiles. A police officer yesterday, a burglar today: who'd have thought?

A couple of chickens die of their injuries, but the others grow up healthily in Patty's back garden. They're taken around primary schools, representing the billions of chickens that are raised in dreadful conditions and slaughtered for human consumption worldwide every year.

There's an ancient Jewish saying: 'Save one life and you save the world.' After the open rescue I believe that applies just as much to animals. We may have violated the law, but it felt great. I want more. Luckily the hunger is about to be satisfied by Sea Shepherd.

In early February the *Steve Irwin* returns to port to restock. Along with dozens of other supporters, I wait on the quayside for the flagship to arrive. We work day and night to get the vessel ready for the second leg of its campaign. A couple of days later, the activists head back to the Japanese hunters in Antarctica. They wave excitedly at those remaining on shore. This time I'm waving too.

06

SEASICKNESS

The ship is deserted. Less than 24 hours into our voyage the *Steve Irwin* seems devoid of life. The corridors are empty, nobody's working on deck and even the mess, where you'll always find some crew members, has been abandoned. The only sign of activity comes from the galley. Laura Dakin is preparing a meal for the handful of crew members who might turn up for breakfast.

'It's the same every year,' she says with a wry smile. She too is suffering the first symptoms. 'The first couple of days are the worst. You won't see a soul. Then the seasickness subsides, if you're lucky that is. I've been on campaigns where the crew was sick for weeks. I hope it won't happen again this year. You could end up in bed all day, unable to keep your food down and, in the worst case, on a drip.'

The chef is standing with her legs apart, knees bent and hips leaning against the worktop. With one hand she clutches the worktop, with the other she stirs a huge pot of baked beans. Her legs move in sync with the ship's roll.

After our festive departure from Melbourne, we crossed Port Phillip Bay and set course for Tasmania. Right now the ship is sailing through the Bass Strait, where two gulf streams collide in the relatively shallow water, causing the *Steve Irwin* to bounce around in a sea of steep, choppy waves. Ideal conditions for seasickness.

I thought I'd escaped the clutches of seasickness. Save for the unpleasant lurch in my stomach with every downward motion, it hasn't given me any trouble so far. But now the smell of baked beans and freshly baked bread turns against me. 'I'm going to get some fresh air,' I tell Laura. She carries on cooking, quite unruffled.

Wearing my best poker face, so as not to let on that I'm starting to feel seasick, I edge out of the galley. But then I sprint to the staircase leading up to the deck. Running on a ship: not advisable. While I'm taking the first few steps, the ship lurches to port and I lose my balance, slip and bang my head hard against the steps. Result: a big bump on my forehead and still very queasy. Cautiously, using both hands for support, I shuffle along the narrow corridor leading to the afterdeck. Fresh air. Too late, the bile is coming up. Quick, the railing! The vomit sticks in my gullet. Don't give in, Lau, don't give in. It's all in the mind, stare at the horizon. The straight line in the distance helps me regain my sense of balance and the nausea gradually subsides. This is when I notice Rob Garcia standing beside me. He's leaning over the railing, puking his guts out. When all that's coming out are some long strands of bile, he wipes his mouth on his sleeve and gasps for breath. 'Good morning mate.' He gives me a toothy grin. 'This wasn't in the recruitment brochure, was it?'

Rob is a hard worker, a rough diamond. His arms are covered in fading tattoos he had done during his teenage years. The three dots between his thumb and index finger were self-inflicted in secondary school. He's not an activist, not even a vegetarian. In fact, with his bald pate, heavy build and coarse ink he looks harder than many a criminal I've come across. And with his Spanish temperament, he gives the impression he's ready to land a right hook at the slightest provocation.

He thinks whales are gorgeous creatures and he wants to show them to his daughter one day. That's the only reason he wants to protect them. Some on board a Sea Shepherd vessel have hundreds of reasons for wanting to protect the whales. Rob has just the one. Simple. He wants to prove to his child that he can make a difference. Having fled a tough life on shore, unable to escape his past, the Spaniard is a black sheep looking to redeem himself. All that matters here on board is that you're a hard worker; it's a kind of foreign legion of passionate conservationists. Rob fits right in: 'roll up your sleeves and get busy' has been his motto for years. And as soon as someone's idle for five minutes, he starts chatting about his many years in the construction industry. Everybody's got to hear Rob's story, though nobody pays him the slightest bit of attention. Now, within less than 24 hours, he's been silenced by the sea. Neptune, who doesn't give a fig about posturing, comes down hard on anybody with a big mouth. Rob's grin is gone again. He turns to face the water, wretched and groaning something about heading back to dry land. We've been at sea for less than a day.

The vomiting sounds beside me aren't exactly conducive to my own recovery, so I start back to my cabin. Halfway, I pass ship's photographer Noah, my mate from Animal Liberation Victoria, who's on his hands and knees, crawling to the toilets. His face is green and splotchy. With his imposing physique, he reminds me of a sad Hulk. He moans and glances at me before quickly turning his vacant gaze back to the toilet block. I keep going and hear the unstoppable splash of vomit hitting the toilet bowl behind me. It's the photographer's first stint at sea.

My cabin is in the front section of the ship. All new recruits start at the front, because it's the worst place on board the *Steve Irwin*. Thank heavens I'm spared the zero-gravity room: the very front cabin is a true torture chamber. While each upward motion of the ship propels you out of your bed, each drop sends you into free fall. Besides, the room is situated beside the anchor cables. Even on calm days, the sound of the clanging chains keeps you awake. Everybody feels sorry for the person at the front, but nobody is prepared to swap.

There are two rooms between my cabin and the zero-gravity room. Not so bad, but my room-mate Alex and I do feel the aftershocks of the clanking. Alex is lying on the lower bunk, hugging a bucket as though he's just been reunited with a long-lost teddy bear and all the happy childhood memories associated with it. His head is hanging over the rim and he hasn't even bothered to wipe away the slime on his chin. Alex begs me to put him out of his misery. My room-mate tries to conjure a smile, but all he can muster is a pained grimace.

'Get well soon,' I try to make it sound as sympathetic as possible. I draw strength from other people's suffering. Neptune won't beat this landlubber.

Having spent the past couple of hours refusing to give in to the nausea, I'm starting to get used to my newly acquired sea legs. Big mugs of ginger tea, no coffee, and fixing my gaze on the horizon every time I feel the urge to vomit are what keeps me going. Seasickness, the first obstacle en route to the whalers, appears to be conquered.

This Sea Shepherd campaign is my first proper voyage at sea. Save for a ferry crossing to England and a fishing trip on the Oosterschelde estuary with colleagues from the police force, my personal logbook doesn't feature any noteworthy sea travels.

Two more days on the Tasman Sea and then we'll hit a real ocean: the Southern Ocean. Mighty waves and ferocious winds, feared by seamen the world over, have free rein here because there's no land below 40 degrees. With each degree of latitude, the descriptions of the powerful winds become more ominous. It kicks off with the 'roaring forties', which greet us after the 40th degree of latitude. In days gone by, the area was favoured by sailing vessels travelling from Australia to Europe, but nowadays it's plied only by adventurers and ships heading for the Antarctic.

The peril duly increases with every 10 degrees we descend. The 'furious fifties' and 'screaming sixties' are awe-inspiring names, complemented by veterans' tall tales about towering waves, raging storms and floating icebergs that will greet us before we get to the ice of Antarctica. For the time being, very few crew members are giving it a second thought. A small group of dyed-in-the-wool seamen keep the ship going. Those of the new recruits who feel well enough are told to start cleaning the toilets and scrubbing the floors. The rest are left to fight the seasickness alone. Those afflicted are going through a hell of puking and struggling to balance organs, while the body gets used to the rolling sea. There's no way out, there's no medicine: it's a question of vomiting or adjusting. You can yell as much as you like, but nobody will come and help. Except, that is, the ship's doctor, who will pop in every now and then to check that you're not becoming dehydrated. Welcome to the high seas. Sea Shepherd campaign Operation Migaloo is underway.

07

THE FIRST WHALE

Seven short blasts on the ship's horn, followed by a long one that keeps reverberating. Evacuation alarm! We all grab our survival suits and rush to the afterdeck, which, according to the emergency procedures disseminated throughout the ship, is our gathering point. Outside, second mate Peter Hammarstedt is waiting for us. Luckily it's just a drill, but with everybody assembled on deck, except for a couple of people on duty on the bridge or in the engine room, the officer seizes the opportunity for a safety briefing.

'If you fall overboard, you're dead,' Peter begins his address. 'The Antarctic waters are merciless. If you're lucky, you've got two minutes before hypothermia sets in. Our ship needs at least 15 minutes to turn round. You do the maths.' He looks stoic as he says it. The veteran has been sailing with Sea Shepherd since he was 17 and he knows the score. A couple of life rafts are rolled up in white canisters over by the helicopter deck, he continues. Only the captain is authorised to order evacuation in the event of an accident, and if he's no longer available, the first mate. Nodding furiously, the crew absorb the safety instructions.

A ship is an accident waiting to happen. It's something most of us became painfully aware of as the *Steve Irwin* was hurled back and forth in the stormy weather of the past few days.

Peter calls out the names of the crew members who are earmarked for the port or the starboard life rafts if the ship were to go down. There are 32 of us: 24 men and 8 women. Eleven are veterans who have been on one or more campaigns, the rest are new recruits. The ten different countries represented here are New Zealand, Australia, the United States, Canada, South Africa, the Netherlands, Spain, Japan, Sweden and Great Britain.

We've had to take everything from our cabin, but a quick count reveals there aren't enough survival suits. The problem is made light of with the announcement that those without an immersion suit should put on a Mustang coverall. The immersion suit takes forever to put on, and you can move much more freely in the yellow Mustang outfit. That's all very well, but just to be on the safe side I'm going to keep an eye on the survival suit in my cabin. Forewarned is forearmed, especially after the threatening waves of the past few nights.

Those with a survival suit are told to put it on over their clothes. When we've finally extracted the stiff, elastic red suits from their covers, we find that many are either too big or too small, so we have to swap between ourselves to find one the right size.

'Hey, I look like a lobster,' Alex says. The fresh air has revived my room-mate, who'd been half-dead on his bed only a few hours ago. The red suit has a tight hood and sleeves that taper to allow space for four fingers and a thumb. Alex walks up and down the deck like a robot, followed by one of the ship's cooks copying his movements. They're fooling around while most of us still haven't got our suits on after five minutes. As long as there's no real danger, the novices don't take the safety drill too seriously. For some volunteers this trip is no more than an adventurous interlude: a spot of whale protection and then home again. The yearning for adventure is all too obvious. Of course we have a clear goal and that's to protect the whales from illegal Japanese hunters. But the thought of reaching the elusive South Pole, the land of penguins and temperatures of more than 90 degrees below zero, where human life is all but impossible, makes my heart beat faster. As a child I did presentations at school about Antarctica; now I'm on my dream journey.

Peter lets the survival suits blunder on, at least for now. After days of seasickness, this opportunity to blow off steam is a welcome distraction. Once the dressing-up party has culminated into a crazy lobster dance, Peter brings the safety drill to an end. He concludes by saying that it's essential for everybody to abide by the rules. The second mate singles out a few of them: be punctual, don't run, always listen to your team leader, keep an eye out for your colleagues, stick to a vegan diet, no smoking and, above all, no drinking. That last rule is received with some grumbling. Peter responds by saying that drowned men regularly wash ashore with their zips undone. In a drunken moment, they decided to piss over the railing and went flying overboard. Whether or not there's any truth in this nautical legend is anyone's guess, but it certainly drives home the need for prohibition.

The safety briefing over, everybody reports to their team leader for the work schedule. Daniel Bebawi, the bosun in charge of the deckhands, explains that our duties are simple. Breakfast is at 8.00, followed by a briefing at 8.30. Then we move on to sweeping the floors, mopping the corridors, scrubbing the toilets and showers or helping out with the washing-up – something different every day. The schedule's drawn up by the bosun. The deck team is also responsible for maintenance and repairs, such as greasing doors, painting and polishing brassware. Not the best job in the world, but a reward awaits us outside: the dinghies. Deckhands prepare the RIBs, handle the lines, launch the boats and are usually physically involved in all the actions. It makes collecting and burning toilet paper more than worth it. Whoever has any time left after completing his daily duties should report to the kitchen, where the cooks can always use a hand.

After a couple of days at sea I'm perfectly happy with my place on the deck team. We spend a great deal of time outside with the wind in our faces; there's no better start to the day than breathing in the fresh sea air. But my job as a deckhand looks set to be short-lived when the engineers announce they're looking for an extra worker. They reckon I might be suitable for the sometimes hectic engine room, that I'm unflappable in the event of an error message. I can't say I fancy it, but before we set off I resolved never to complain and to do whatever I was asked to do. A promise is a promise, so at 7.45 the next morning I report to the engine room. As in the pilothouse, the shifts here are four hours on, eight hours off and then four hours on again.

As soon as the large white door swings open and my colleague sticks his head round it, a little red warning light above the door comes on – it wouldn't be the first time the heavy steel door hit a passer-by in the face. I grab some safety goggles and ear protectors and then we go down a narrow flight of stairs to the control room.

I find myself blinking at dozens and dozens of temperature, pressure and speed gauges. I'm feeling less comfortable by the minute among the throbbing engines. Every single gauge is a complete mystery to me, but so as not to look like a complete idiot I nod to suggest that I understand. But after every new controlling device, I've forgotten all about the previous one.

The engine room is windowless. The only light comes from a few fluorescent tubes on the ceiling. And unless you receive communications from the bridge via the internal phone, you've no idea what's going on outside. The sole advantage of this space is that it's the most stable part of the ship. Even in stormy weather, the engine room doesn't roll much.

My supervisor shows me how to top up the oil in the engines. The rancid smell of the diesel fumes is sickening. There's no fresh air in this stuffy space whatsoever. And with the engines roaring non-stop, the engineer has to yell his instructions into my ear. I hate every single minute among the thundering nautical apparatus. But every time I'm forced to dodge yet another boiling hot component that's been soldered into some random place, my respect for the engineers grows.

Even though the team get to set their own working hours, command a lot of respect among the crew and each worker has their own cabin, I don't want to spend a minute longer in this fetid hole after my four-hour ordeal. When the torment is finally over, the engineer asks me kindly: 'What do you think? That wasn't bad for a first time, was it?'

'Well, you know, I don't think it's my cup of tea. I'm someone who likes being out on deck with the wind in my face.'

And I'm not lying. In fact, I'd rather stand on the bow for four hours, stark naked and catching my death from cold, than spend another day in the engine room. But I spare him the aversion and thank him for the interesting introduction. I'd better stay on friendly terms with him, because if he's determined to have me on his team, I'll be spending the entire campaign in the engine room. Fingers crossed that he appreciates my honesty.

I spend the rest of the day with the deck team. The weather is reasonably calm and we all do odd jobs on deck. Together with Daniel and a couple of others, Rob practises with the hydraulic crane. He picks up empty oil barrels and tries to set them down again elsewhere on the deck. Two other volunteers grease the door lock mechanisms, while yet another repairs the rope ladders.

All of a sudden a voice comes on over the loudspeakers on deck. 'Whales on starboard side.' We all stop what we're doing and look to the bridge. Four guys rush outside and point to the water. 'Whales. Whales!' the quartermasters yell excitedly. Everybody on deck hurries over to the bow to catch a glimpse of the animals. I've never seen a whale and work my way to the front.

Two finbacks. Their elongated backs are visible as they glide through the water. As soon as the whales exhale, a blowhole expels a big cloud of water drops. Sunlight transforms the spray into a gorgeous rainbow hovering for several seconds above the giant mammals. This is the first time I've seen these enormous creatures in the flesh. They're more impressive than I ever imagined.

Japan has 50 of these finbacks on its hit list. In addition, they're planning to harpoon 935 minke whales. They're also keen to capture 50 humpbacks, but may be willing to forgo this after diplomatic pressure from Australia. And all this under the guise of 'science'.

Not all that long ago, the oceans were full of whales. The wonderful spectacle of whales frolicking off the coast was just as common as screeching gulls in the skies above the beach. In open seas the gigantic mammals swam together in huge numbers, fulfilling their role in the fragile ecosystem of the oceans.

That was until countries such as Japan, and many western European countries, discovered industrial whaling. They piled onto steamships and hunted the giant mammals in their droves. Whales seemed like the perfect catch. Everything was used: meat for consumption, oil for fuel, fat and liver oil for food supplements. Even the bones were used for things like cutlery, corsets and picture frames.

But there was worse to come after World War II. Years of conflict had led to a shortage of fat and protein. Offering plenty of both, the gigantic whales seemed like the obvious solution, and so they were caught in huge numbers to provide hungry people with food. Worldwide, the whale population declined at an extraordinary rate because stocks were not being given the chance to replenish. In 1986, when it was almost too late, the international community introduced a moratorium on commercial whaling. While no species had become extinct yet, the huge mammals had all but disappeared off the coasts.

Most countries observed the fishing ban. Japan, on the other hand, went looking for new hunting grounds. The country saw a fantastic opportunity in the seas around Antarctica. More than 2 million whales had been slaughtered there over the past century, but Japan couldn't care less. After the blue whale had mostly disappeared, the harpoons began targeting sperm whales. And when they'd all been killed, the finbacks faced a similar fate. No species was safe from the predatory whalers. One after the other, the whale species around Antarctica were brought to the brink of extinction. And Japan couldn't care less.

With all the other major whale species breathing their last, the Japanese government began to shift its focus to the minke whale. But because of the moratorium issued by the International Whaling Commission, it had to come up with a loophole for the massacre. The answer: science. A clause in the fishing ban states that whales may be caught for scientific purposes. There are no limits on these so-called 'scientific catches'; countries are allowed to decide for themselves how many cetaceans they want to catch.

Without any sanctioning powers, the commission is a bit of a joke anyway. The Japanese Institute for Cetacean Research concluded that in order to carry out serious research it had to catch more than a thousand whales in the Antarctic. To lend the whole story some credibility, the spin doctors had to modify the terminology. Commercial whaling was scrapped from the dictionaries and replaced with scientific-sounding terminology; words aimed at misleading the public. The spin doctors had clearly heeded Joseph Goebbels, the Nazi propaganda minister who once said that it's not the truth that matters, but what the people believe to be the truth.

And so it happened. The 8,000 tonne factory ship *Nisshin Maru*, onto which the whales are loaded before being hacked to pieces, became the mother ship for cetacean research. The harpoon vessels, which, when the opportunity arises, shoot an explosive device into the whales and rip the animals apart from the inside, became sample-taking ships. The rare harpoons that missed their targets were dubbed failed samples by Japan. A cut-up and frozen minke whale wasn't whale meat, but a by-product of research. And those by-products could be sold on the market after the research was completed. Japan had found a solution.

The world turns a blind eye to what's going on. And because the Whaling Commission doesn't have the power to impose penalties, nobody is taking any action against this Japanese pseudo-research. Nobody, except the 31 volunteers who are now on the bow of the *Steve Irwin*, cheering the colossal finbacks like little children.

That evening we celebrate seeing our first whales. In a day or two we'll reach the Antarctic, so we know that this may be one of our last chances to relax. A small group of us have gathered in a cabin. The room is no bigger than 2 by 3 metres, but to my surprise it actually holds more than 10 people. Everybody is squashed together, sitting on each other's laps or leaning against something or other. We're listening to the veterans' hair-raising stories, with Bob Dylan singing 'The Times They are a-Changin'' in the background. One of the deckhands pulls a pack of beers from under the bed. The ban on alcohol is still in place, but there's an unwritten rule among the crew that everybody smuggles some booze on board. A rule that the new recruits were unaware of.

Now we have no option but to take advantage of the veterans' generosity. Well, drinking on your own is no fun, so in no time at all the young buccaneers are swigging from a can of lager, and a hipflask filled with whisky is passed round as a nightcap. With a little booze inside the jolly green pirates, the volume inside the cabin increases exponentially. Bob Dylan has been replaced by Irish folk musicians and now 'Whiskey in the Jar' is blasting from the small stereo. We're all singing along at the top of our voices when the door of the cabin swings open, banging hard against the bunk bed. 'What the hell is going on here?' Peter yells furiously. Normally officers don't venture below decks, but the second mate was looking for his girlfriend Amber when he heard the laughter and noise.

The beers are stashed away under cushions and mattresses. 'Just chilling,' we say in unison. Peter is about to launch into a sermon, but before he has a chance to open his mouth he spots Amber among us. He goes red in the face and stammers that any minute now we could run into the whaling fleet. We must be ready for action at all times. Every crew member in the room knows that the moment is at least two more days away, but we all think it's best to keep our mouths shut. The officer marches off in a huff. Amber leaps to her feet and, clearly embarrassed, runs after her boyfriend. We slowly shuffle out of the cabin. Now that our clandestine gathering has been detected nobody wants to carry on boozing.

With a big grin on my face, I stagger back to my berth. Tiresome chores, insufficient equipment (and what we do have urgently needs replacing), volunteers who can't tell their arse from their elbow, superiors who are greener than grass, and yet the *Steve Irwin* is sailing 24 hours a day, heading steadily towards the whaling fleet. The crew are a motley bunch, but they're an incredibly passionate motley bunch. This is the life. There's nowhere I'd rather be.

08

CRAZY IVAN

As soon as we pass the Antarctic Convergence zone a bitter cold descends on the ship. The first few icebergs float by on our left and right. The novices among us thought that the icebergs the size of a small house were colossal. But after two days in the South Pole region we begin to realise that, compared with the enormous tower blocks of ice floating past right now, those initial bergs were mere pebbles.

With our arrival in Antarctica comes a spanner in the works: the *Fukuyoshi Maru No. 68*. The Japanese patrol ship has a single objective: to trace the *Steve Irwin* and pass our position on to the fleet, so it can keep out of our way. Since the Japanese vessel is keeping a respectable distance of 11 miles, we're within their radar range but too far to take action. The Fukuyoshi can easily do 22 knots, as opposed to our 15. They won't have any trouble avoiding us.

The latest from the pilothouse is that, in spite of our pursuer, we're some 70 sea miles closer to the whaling fleet. According to our intelligence, the fleet has changed direction slightly and is now heading north. Captain Watson estimates that we're about 90 sea miles from the factory ship: a stone's throw in this vast ocean.

After the day's update I go outside with a cup of tea. I really enjoy looking at the calm sea. The water is smooth at the moment, but the gentle breeze that picks up creates ripples on the surface.

Weather conditions can change from one minute to the next in Antarctica and so they do: just before noon, the *Steve Irwin* is ploughing through a strong gale. Big waves wash over the deck and freeze within seconds to form a thin layer of ice. The wind whips past the ship like crazy and engulfs the rubber boats in sleet. Waves collide and push each other to ominous heights. When they reach their peak they burst into a plume of seawater. The frozen spray hits the windows of the bridge, from where the first mate is peering out. Rising mist reduces visibility to just a couple of hundred metres. Our pursuer is still 10 miles behind us.

First mate Peter Brown thinks this is a good time for a Crazy Ivan. Although the strategy dates back to the Cold War, when the oceans were teeming with American and Russian submarines, it's perfect for this present-day cold war. During the arms race between East and West the main players were constantly threatening attack. The Russians were always looking nervously over their shoulder to check for American submarines, and would regularly do a U-turn. This would force a pursuer to slam on the brakes, making a noise that was easily picked up by the Soviet sonar. Peter now wants to use this simple trick to shake off the Japanese ship. He puts the helm over and charges at the *Fukuyoshi*, which is blithely heading our way. The Japanese don't notice us until we're only half a mile away. Their captain has a terrible shock and yanks the whaler to port. With the engines at full throttle, a thick plume of black smoke rises up. Panic-stricken, the hunter scurries east. Before long the distance between both vessels is more than 10 miles.

Captain Watson doesn't think twice and navigates the *Steve Irwin* through an ice field – highly dangerous for a vessel without an ice class, but Watson has years of experience at sea. We sail through the mist without taking excessive risks. Every time the captain comes across an iceberg that's several times the size of the *Steve Irwin*, he switches the engines off. Without a sound, we float past the giant. On the radar, our vessel vanishes in a field of ice. Our pursuer will never find us here, Watson reckons.

As quickly as it got up, the storm dies down again. There's not a breath of wind now, and with the temperature just below freezing it's almost pleasant outside. Our ship is bobbing in the perfectly smooth water and will be drifting here until we're certain that we've shaken off the *Fukuyoshi* and we're free to resume our pursuit of the factory ship.

The imposed moment of rest prompts an idiotic, but time-honoured tradition: this is the perfect moment to get some first-hand experience of the icy Antarctic water. It's time for the Penguin Plunge. Those brave enough to take the plunge will receive a certificate from the captain afterwards. The only snag: no protective clothing. Swimming trunks for the men and a swimming costume for the women are all that's allowed.

Seven crew members are giving it a go. If thousands of Dutch people can brave the sea at Scheveningen on New Year's Day, I obviously can't pass up this opportunity at the South Pole. A belated New Year's Day swim as it were. I have to uphold my country's honour.

The heavy door in the ship's bulwark is opened and a rope ladder lowered down the side. The participants are shivering on the fore-deck. A few whirling snowflakes prove that it's still freezing cold.

Jeff Hansen is the first to jump off the rope ladder. The spectators have barely had a chance to blink before he's back on deck, dripping wet. 'Fucking freezing,' the tough Australian mutters through blue lips. Clear language.

Alex goads me into doing something a bit bolder than just jumping off the rope ladder. He's right. I walk to the edge of the ship, hesitate a second, but then dive into the Southern Ocean with my arms spread wide. While in the air I yell: 'Who wants to live forever?!' I promised my brother I'd let out this fatalistic yell at some point during the campaign. This is the right moment.

When my forehead hits the icy water it feels as though a nail is being driven into my skull. The sharp pain passes through my whole body until I come back up, spluttering. I gasp for air, but the cold is so intense I almost hyperventilate. Out, out, my instinct tells me. The way up is tortuous, because the cold has paralysed my limbs. On deck I flail my arms about while trying to drape myself in a proffered towel.

'Your turn,' I grin at Alex. He takes a run-up, but slips just before he reaches the edge. His legs go out from under him and he plummets upside-down into the water. He lands heavily on his back. We all peer over the railing, anxious to see if he resurfaces. Luckily, my room-mate emerges relatively unscathed from the free fall of several metres. He's close to tears. His back is all red and blue and he's groaning with pain. But while he's rubbing his body, the *Schadenfreude* is taking the edge off my headache.

After a brief shower, I hear the latest news. The floating slaughterhouse *Nisshin Maru* is steaming eastwards. The distance between us is approximately 120 sea miles. We're sailing somewhere parallel to the Australian Casey Station on the mainland. According to our calculations, the Japanese whaler will shortly have to refuel at the *Oriental Bluebird*. This enormous supply ship is sailing somewhere north of us. The ships will have to be at anchor to transfer fuel and provisions. We're hoping that this will give us a chance to close in. And they will have to link up soon, because a violent autumn storm is approaching from the north. The *Bluebird* will want to avoid it. Since we're approaching from the west and Antarctica's treacherous ice awaits in the south, the *Nisshin* can only go east.

If the Japanese do decide to set course for the north, we'll cut them off. And as long as they're running away from us, they're not catching any whales. We may not actually have the whalers in our sights, but we know that while we're chasing them they'll never meet their fishing quota.

09

GOTCHA!

The many discomforts of the spartan lifestyle on board the *Steve Irwin* no longer matter. Any irritations among the crew have been pushed to the background and the challenge of living in the pockets of strangers for weeks is finally paying off: we have located the Japanese whaling fleet.

At around 14.00 hours on 2 March we come within reach of the hunters. As soon as the harpoon ships realise we're near they scatter every which way. Luckily the crew of the *Steve Irwin* has been paying attention, because we're setting course for the big, slow-moving silhouette fleeing south. The distance between us is about 15 miles. The *Nisshin Maru* has a top speed of around 13 to 15 knots, depending on its cargo. Our top speed is between 14 and 15 knots. Catching up will require a lot of patience from the crew.

On our way south, we pass gigantic icebergs. Low-lying clouds catch the light reflecting off them, creating a mysterious glow; we're entering a new, magical landscape.

But not for long, as the *Nisshin Maru* soon veers north. Relief all round, because growlers – floating chunks of ice, some of which are as big as a Volkswagen Beetle and almost invisible on the radar – are a lot less common in the north. Now that it's March, the days are getting shorter and it's becoming increasingly difficult to spot these chunks of sea ice.

By the evening the contours of the 8,000 tonne slaughterhouse are more clearly identifiable. It's still far off on the horizon, but the experienced crew would recognise the *Nisshin Maru* anywhere. Now we know for certain we can sabotage the hunt.

Around 23.00 hours I decide to go to bed. Alex, who's working the night shift, has promised to wake me if we get any closer.

At 02.30 hours the *Steve Irwin* is less than a mile from the accursed ship. It's pitch-dark outside. The *Nisshin Maru* can only be identified by a searchlight on its stern. The bright beam scours the water in front of our bow for any suspect activity. I go back to bed to get a few more hours of well-needed sleep because I have a sneaking suspicion that we could be in for a busy day.

At 06.45 hours bosun Daniel bangs on our bedroom door. 'Report to the bridge. We're about to attack!' Captain Watson wants Ralph Lowe and me to kick things off by throwing butyric acid from the bow at the factory ship. If the hunters are cutting up whale meat, we're going to render it unmarketable. The rancid butter will taint the meat so it can't be sold. The more money the fleet loses the better. We're also throwing methylcellulose (methacel). Upon contact with water this powder turns into an extremely slippery substance. While it doesn't stop the whale hunt, it certainly delays it and that's always welcome.

On deck, Peter is handing out the bottles of butyric acid. A couple of the caps have leaked, so the storage container reeks of a mixture of vomit and rotten eggs, and we have to tie a scarf around our faces so as not to gag. Carrying a bucket of butyric acid and methacel, we shuffle to the prow. Let's hope none of the bottles break. Behind us,

Noah is fiddling with his cameras so he can capture our every move. Behind him is a cameraman. Ralph is a paramedic and I'm a former police officer; that's to say, we're not your typical environmental activists. I suspect the captain's hoping for an eye-catching publicity shot. The four of us waddle across the deck like penguins until we reach the prow with all our ammunition.

Meanwhile the *Steve Irwin* is sailing right behind the *Nisshin*. Captain Watson is at the helm, the distance between us no more than 100 metres. Ralph and I are ready. I've taken off one of my gloves to get some sort of grip on the glass, while I'm clutching the railing with my other hand to keep my balance. The Sea Shepherd ship is edging closer: 90 metres, 80, 70. With every metre we advance my heart pounds harder in my chest. Ralph's intent gaze suggests similar nerves. All eyes are on us. This is it.

Captain Watson turns the helm to the left and passes the Japanese processing ship on the port side. Water cannons positioned at the rear and the side of the whaler are aimed at our ship, trying to blow us off the deck. They only just miss us. Out of the drainage holes in the side of the *Nisshin Maru* blood is pouring into the sea; the hunters have managed to catch a whale after all.

From the *Nisshin Maru* we hear a robotic female voice warning us not to jump on board, while on the Japanese deck a couple of men in blue uniforms film our every move. The rest of the personnel have been summoned inside, except for a few hunters on the bridge staring at us through binoculars.

'Now!' Ralph yells. I hesitate. I reckon the distance is too great. Ralph gives it everything he's got and hurls a bottle of butyric acid towards the whaler. All eyes on the ship follow its flight. Alas, the glass shatters against the hull of the *Nisshin Maru*. I signal to the captain to move closer. The *Steve Irwin* edges a couple of metres nearer: we can do it now. On the count of three, we both toss the stinkbombs across. Bullseye. They burst on the Japanese processing deck. A couple more bottles follow, all hitting their target.

Ralph even throws one right up to the pilothouse. The startled hunters flee inside.

The packets of methacel land on the prow. They burst open, releasing a white cloud that slowly drifts across the deck. Along the entire length of our vessel bottles of butyric acid and methacel are now flying towards the factory ship. Almost all of them hit home. The odd bottle ends up in the water or smashes against the side, but most of the smelly substance reaches our adversary. The Japanese ship gives off a terrible stench. The crew is jubilant, high-fiving and hugging each other spontaneously: this foul odour is also the sweet smell of victory.

Following the butyric acid blitz, the *Steve Irwin* drops back behind the *Nisshin Maru*'s slipway. Having bared our teeth for a moment, our ship now blocks the rear so the hunters can't haul any dead whales on board.

The first round goes to Sea Shepherd. The harpoon ships are keeping out of our way, while the factory ship flees north, away from the whale sanctuary. The hunt has ended. The 120-man crew of the *Nisshin Maru* is unable to stop the indomitable volunteers. The ship is in a state of euphoria. We go to bed early, because who knows, we may be launching another attack in a couple of hours.

10

COASTGUARD AND STUN GRENADES

It's been seven days since we first made contact with the floating slaughterhouse from Japan. We've been chasing the ship for more than 2,000 miles, and while we've been in pursuit, no whale has been killed.

Now that autumn is setting in here in Antarctica, the weather is turning grimmer by the day. We won't be able to sail for much longer before having to dip into our fuel reserves. But the prolonged darkness and more frequent storms are further dangers that the *Steve Irwin* can't arm itself against. Only two days ago, our ship was completely covered in a thick layer of ice. And yesterday, nobody was allowed out on the weather deck because of relentless blizzards. And yet the crew isn't bothered: knowing that we've shut down the hunt means we're all in high spirits. The time spent indoors is filled with cooking, tying knots or splitting ropes. Before I came on board, I could only tie a slipknot. After Daniel's masterclasses I can add bowlines, clove hitches and figures of eight to my repertoire.

In a couple of days' time, the Japanese fleet will return to port. Given the good visibility and calm water, today is probably the last chance for them to boost their fishing quota a little. But as long as the *Steve Irwin*'s in pursuit, we won't let them.

Every now and then Captain Watson feigns an attack. The Japanese crew, who have been ordered to stay below decks, are powerless as they watch through the portholes. The odd one gives us the finger, but most of them just peer out of the window, looking glum. And who can blame them? Spending days doing karaoke instead of cutting up whale cadavers isn't quite what they had in mind.

Out on deck are the men in dark-blue uniforms. Through binoculars we read the words 'Coast Guard'. It's actually illegal to bring the police or military into the Antarctic region, but it looks as if Japan is flouting this international agreement.

The smell of butyric acid clings to the *Nisshin Maru* for ages, and to make sure it does over the next couple of days as well, Captain Watson orders another rancid butter attack. Alex, Ralph and I will now be throwing from the monkey deck, the top platform situated above the pilothouse. I can tell I'm tenser than the first time. We have no idea how the uniformed men will react this time.

Our Jolly Roger is fluttering proudly on the bow as we steam ahead for our offensive. This time we're aiming for the whaler's foredeck, so the stench will blow across the rest of the ship. The air vents are another target. It would be great if we could also stink up the interior of the *Nisshin Maru*. The crew is ready. We're thinking back to that one moment which makes every second in this dangerous region worth the trouble.

Yesterday around noon we witnessed the most amazing spectacle many of us will ever see. It began with a couple of rare hourglass dolphins that were riding our bow wave. They lured us to the bow so Mother Nature could reveal her full gift to us: pods of dolphins, long-finned pilot whales, minke whales and humpbacks foraging together. About 100 animals in total, swimming between us and the factory ship. Even the skipper said he'd never seen anything quite like it. While the mammals were swimming around freely, the *Nisshin Maru* beat its retreat in the background. If Sea Shepherd hadn't been sailing here, the Japanese whaling fleet would have caused a bloodbath, no doubt about it. But not now. Now the giants of the sea were leaping in and out of the water without a care in the world. The humpbacks were swimming right beside our ship, occasionally rolling onto their sides to have a look at the cheering idiots on the deck. They flapped their tails before disappearing under water for minutes on end.

The commanding officer of the *Nisshin Maru* contacts Captain Watson on channel 16 on our radio. The message is clear: Sea Shepherd must cease its actions, or the Japanese coastguard will deploy teargas and stun grenades. Watson doesn't think twice: 'Sea Shepherd is upholding international laws flouted by Japan. Japan is operating illegally in Antarctic waters and Sea Shepherd will not be threatened by a band of poachers. Japan has no right to deploy weapons against an unarmed marine crew.' He pulls no punches. We all keep a nervous eye on the frantic movements of the officers on board the factory ship.

We're drawing closer to the factory ship. The wind has picked up and the snow sweeps across our faces. On the main deck, the windchill factor has now dipped well below zero. We're freezing cold. Alex and I are complaining bitterly about the piercing cold that's flagellating our limbs. 'What did you expect? This is Antarctica!' Ralph remarks drily.

A little closer still. Judging by the faces of the Japanese coastguard stationed on deck, they really mean it this time. My heart is pounding. We psych ourselves up: 'We're doing it for the whales. We're acting lawfully. Japan's committing an offence. We have to protect these animals.'

From the bridge Peter signals that we won't be going any closer. My bottle of butyric acid sails through the air. Immediately afterwards a voice behind me yells: 'Incoming!' A black ball comes hurtling through the air towards me. In a reflex I duck and hear a loud blast beside me. My ears are ringing and for a couple of seconds the voices of the other throwers sound far away.

The coastguard is lobbing stun grenades, also known as flashbangs, which are used by police squads on land to disorientate suspects prior to arrest. This may well be the first time weapons are being deployed in Antarctica. It's given us a fright, but we refuse to be put out. Butyric acid and methacel go flying towards the *Nisshin Maru*. Again, the *Nisshin*'s captain comes over the radio, telling us to halt our actions. Captain Watson responds by saying that they're the ones using illegal weapons and that they should piss off and leave the whale sanctuary. Neither party will concede.

Meanwhile the *Nisshin* is diverting to a bank of fog. The wind is picking up, whipping the waves to ominous heights. But still the *Steve Irwin* pushes on, determined to get to the whale hunter. We're so close now that both our bow waves shoot up the ships' sides and into the air like geysers, showering us with a spray of ice water.

On the monkey deck Peter hands round the last few packets of methacel and bottles of butyric acid. With the wind trying to knock us off the deck, we have to hold on tight. The Japanese coastguard watch us approach. Our eyes meet. We keep staring at each other. Nobody looks away. We're showing them that we're not giving in to violent intimidation. We're here for the thousands of whales slaughtered by Japan in recent decades. Today justice will prevail.

Methacel sails across and bursts on the whaler's deck. Three, four flashbangs head our way. The grenades are now aimed directly at us and explode less than a metre away. They're immediately followed by another load of flashbangs. An exploding stun grenade lands on Ralph's back. He screams with pain and scrambles for cover. Despite a constant high-pitched ringing in our ears, we're hanging in there.

After every grenade we get back on our feet and hurl our missiles at the whaler until their deck is littered with bottles of butyric acid and becomes slippery from all the methacel.

When the methacel and butyric acid are all gone, the Sea Shepherd vessel moves away from the *Nisshin Maru*. The factory ship is giving off an unbelievable stench, which we hope will linger long enough to stop the whalers from hunting.

Suddenly, a crew member on the bridge yells that Captain Watson has been hit. In the pilothouse, half the ship has gathered around our commanding officer, who's staring wanly at a small hole in his Mustang suit. The ship's doctor extricates a piece of lead. Among the chaos of the incoming stun grenades, Paul has been hit by something that looks a lot like a bullet. His bulletproof vest stopped the projectile. The Japanese government refuses to respond to the incident, even after the campaign. Likewise the Australian Federal Police won't be drawn into the delicate matter. It's a bizarre and profoundly sad finale to a confrontation between people fighting for life and compassion, and people without any respect for their fellow human beings or indeed any living creatures.

The *Steve Irwin* trails the whaler for several more days. But another confrontation proves unnecessary: the bad weather makes hunting impossible. And according to the forecast, conditions aren't set to improve. The whale hunt is over for this season. On the last of its fuel, the *Steve Irwin* limps back to Australia.

11

THE BEGGARS OF ANTARCTICA

Operation Migaloo is over. It won't be long now before we set foot on land again and everyday life welcomes us back into its fold. On deck, we're all having our final moment with the Southern Ocean. Some are staring glassy-eyed across the vast water, lost in thought. Others are enjoying the breeze and admiring the beauty of the clear blue environment that's been their world for the past few weeks. An environment I've come to appreciate immensely. During life at sea, minutes feel like hours and hours like days. Within this eternity you tend to reflect, longer than you would on land, on those moments when nature shows you a glimpse of her immeasurable beauty.

Sometimes, in the dead of night, I'd stare for hours at the infinite star-studded sky where green polar light danced to the roll of the waves. And there were moments I'd lose myself in the flight of the albatross soaring graciously over the choppy water, which formed a new landscape with every swell. Life at sea proves that if you take the time for inconsequential moments there's a chance they will grow into pearls. It may have been nature's way of thanking this small group of volunteers who were taking the trouble to protect her creatures.

Hundreds of whales were spared thanks to the efforts of 33 volunteers. Every single one of these people made a personal sacrifice to be part of this campaign. Some volunteers gave up their jobs or used up all their holiday allowance for this mission. Others had set aside money for years. And last but not least, we'd all had to say goodbye to loved ones to join this risky battle against the illegal Japanese whaling fleet.

The resulting crew was a melting pot of backgrounds and nationalities. Computer experts, doctors, electricians, paramedics, mechanics and cooks, to name but a few examples, travelled from all over the world to Melbourne to sail with Sea Shepherd. And what began as a mere adventure developed into a truly meaningful mission.

While I was reading some articles branding the Sea Shepherd crew ecoterrorists, I cast my mind back to my history lessons at secondary school. In the sixteenth century a group of Dutchmen escaped the atrocities perpetrated by the Spanish oppressors in the Netherlands. This band of rebels gathered in Dover and, with little in the way of resources, went out to fight the inquisition. From their base at sea, the Dutch pirates drove the Spaniards out of city after Dutch city. Terrorists or freedom fighters? To me the answer was clear. My work with Sea Shepherd in the South Pole region felt similar. With few resources, the pirates of compassion did everything they could to chase the pirates of greed out of the whale sanctuary in the Southern Ocean.

The Geuzen, or Beggars, drove out the occupiers, our crew the Japanese. I could only be incredibly proud of the international crowd I'd worked with over the past month. For weeks, they sacrificed all else and fought for the protection of the living treasures of the ocean. Opponents may brand my fellow fighters ecoterrorists, but I would always think of them as the Beggars of Antarctica.

Operation Migaloo came to encompass more than the protection of whales alone. To me, the campaign came to symbolise all endangered species in the world. There are laws, regulations and international treaties that protect the baleen whales, and yet every year hundreds of these endangered animals are ripped to pieces by harpoons. Not a single organisation, not a single authority, not a single country has done anything to uphold the legislation, except the Sea Shepherd Conservation Society, an organisation that won't be intimidated by an economic superpower. This is an organisation I want to support for many more years to come, and help it get bigger and deploy more vessels. If mankind fails to protect rare whales then that seals the fate of all endangered animal species as far as I'm concerned, from European hamster to Rwandan mountain gorilla, from badger to snow leopard, from tuna to Andean condor. They will all be doomed.

In the end, our battle with the whaling fleet saved 500 whales. The Japanese Institute for Cetacean Research released these official figures when the ships returned to port. But the battle for justice hasn't been won yet. Far from it. The whalers want to raise their fishing quota. In fact, there are rumours about a new processing ship. Whatever happens, as soon as Japan hoists its flag and sets sail for Antarctica again, Sea Shepherd will be in hot pursuit.

I wanted to be part of the next campaign. This year I only got a sniff of the action. Every time the deckhands eased the ropes and launched the rubber boats, there was only one thing I wanted: to sit in one of those boats, to sabotage the work of the harpoon ships and put a stop to the cannons.

I wanted to be there disrupting the whale hunt and proving, once more, that everybody can change this world for the better, no matter how bizarre the challenge or how big your opponent. As long as you really want to; as long as you take that first step.

THE ADVENTURE

" We ourselves feel that what we are doing is just a drop in the ocean. But the ocean would be less because of that missing drop.
MOTHER TERESA "

12

KUNG FU IN MELBOURNE

Ralph's balled fist hits me square in the face. I stagger back a couple of steps as shooting pains replace the boxing glove that's just landed on my chin. You lowered your hands, the Chinese grandmaster Cheung snaps at me. You ought to step aside a lot faster when your opponent takes a swing at you. That's all he says. Training, training and yet more training is all that matters if I want to become an instructor. There's no point in talking about a martial art. He walks off and lights a joss stick under a photo of Ip Man, the founder of Wing Chun kung fu.

The aroma of sandalwood fills the dojo while the grandmaster grumbles that the school has too few pupils. The man is my teenage hero, a living legend, an undisputed heavyweight in the world of martial arts. For that reason alone, the school ought to be full to the rafters every day.

As a child William Cheung trained with Bruce Lee and fought with gangs on the streets of Hong Kong until he was forced to flee abroad. During the passage to Australia he fought other emigrants and hoodlums and eventually made it to the top of the pecking order. In the 1970s and 1980s he became world famous and founded his own Worldwide Wing Chun Kung Fu Association. The school in Melbourne was meant to become a kung fu palace.

But fame is transitory. With other martial arts in the ascendant, the kung fu master became less popular. He was left a broken man, albeit one with great fighting skills. Fighting was the only thing he could do, both physically and verbally.

This was reflected in his method of teaching: strict discipline and subservience to the teacher. The latter, in particular, didn't sit well with the Australian 'Oy, take it easy mate' mentality or with my level-headed Dutch 'Who do you think you are?' upbringing. It wasn't uncommon for the grandmaster to fly into a wild rage whenever a student dared to say more than 'yes, sigung'. The dojo, which offered five training sessions a day, was never filled to capacity.

Ralph, the head instructor and my sparring partner, hits the side of my head guard. 'Come on, keep going.' He makes a feint, and once again I closely follow his athletic body as it moves across the mat. I take a couple of swings at him, plant a fine kick in his side and become painfully aware which one of us is the better fighter. Thirty minutes later I leave the dojo, knackered, on my last legs and covered in bruises. Ralph is a true warrior. He never gives up. If I ever had to choose someone to be by my side in a dangerous situation, I'd go for Ralph.

After my training session, the grandmaster bosses me about: 'The kitchen needs cleaning. Have you checked the merchandise? Have the orders been dispatched? Empty the bins. Call the defaulters. Hoover the dojo. Do the shittiest jobs I can think of.' OK, he didn't literally say that last bit, but it's what I thought when the Wing Chun master bore down on me yet again.

The only thing that keeps me going is the knowledge that this job is temporary. My mind's on the next Sea Shepherd campaign.

As soon as I get the call, I'm off. I'm only doing these training sessions to be as fit as possible for when I'm allowed back on that ship. It's all I can think of, to be honest, and that fills me with a huge emptiness. Clinging to dreams leaves no room for reality. I don't bother making plans for the future with my girlfriend, because whatever happens I'm going back on campaign. This year, next year, whenever, I don't care. I'm obsessed by the prospect of adventure and campaigning.

It's hard to explain to someone who's never experienced a campaign. The voyage across the ocean, the camaraderie, the confrontation between good and evil, the unspoilt wilderness of Antarctica: no matter how vivid my stories, they're no more than anecdotes to my friends and family; adventurous but nothing special.

This is what it must be like for a soldier returning from the battlefield. A period of recognition when you come home, maybe a measure of respect from those around you, but then the bubble which had you thinking you did the most important job in the world suddenly bursts. Too bad mate, after a couple of days everybody has all but forgotten about your experiences. What follows is a black hole you can only climb out of with the help of fellow fighters who do understand what you're going through. Only a return to the battlefield will heal the festering wound of a memory that outshines whatever's happening today.

Finally, in October 2008, I receive the long-awaited email from Peter Hammarstedt:

Hi Laurens,

We'd like to welcome you back on board. The *Steve Irwin* is in Brisbane. If you could join the crew in November, that would be great. Please let us know if you're available.

Best wishes,

Peter

Later that same day, I return my keys to the kung fu school to Grandmaster Cheung's desk. His jeering follows me all the way out the door. Sometimes it's better not to meet your heroes.

13

ROOM FOR THREE

Brisbane, Australia – early November 2008.

The wobbly gangplank scrapes across the concrete quay at the Bulk Sugar Terminal, in sync with the roll of the river. The castor that was already missing last year still hasn't been replaced. The air around the *Steve Irwin* is heavy with drying paint fumes and iron filings. Under the tropical sun, it's boiling hot on the deck of the jet-black ship. I go unnoticed by the crew, who are dressed in sandals, shorts and sweat-soaked T-shirts and who are busy polishing the rust off the stern bulwarks. The deck is littered with paint pots, tools and extension cables, which, if you care to follow them, lead to busy volunteers.

When I caress the rough cladding of the hull, the saline deposits of evaporated seawater cling to my fingertips. I crush the crystals and smell my fingers. The unmistakable salt smell of the sea, followed immediately by the sweet memory of the adventures on the previous Antarctica campaign. God, I've missed this ship.

Inside, bosun Daniel greets me with a big hug. 'Welcome back,' he exclaims. 'You're with us for the whole campaign this year?'

'Absolutely, I'm here to stay.'

'Wait till you see your room.'

'What do you mean?'

Without a word, Daniel leads the way down the stairs towards the bottom deck. My cabin is roughly in the middle of the deck, two rooms on from last year's lodgings; not bad at all. The room is fitted with a bunk bed, a metre-long bench, a washbasin and a small cabinet that my room-mate and I will have to share. The room feels stuffy and close, and is baking hot to boot. Daniel blames it on the faulty air-conditioning that volunteer mechanics have been tinkering with for days but unsuccessfully so far. I'd better get used to it because I'll be sleeping in this sweltering heat for at least another month. We're not setting off for the cold south until early December.

'Wietse, your room-mate, has already claimed the bottom bunk, so if I were you I'd grab the top one before Pottsy arrives.'

'What do you mean, before Pottsy arrives?'

'The ship is full, so we have to improvise. He's joining you. On the floor.'

'There'll be three of us sleeping here? Are you serious?'

'Yes. Still sure you're with us for the whole campaign?' As the bosun walks off chuckling, I'm shocked to see my 1 square metre of personal space shrink to the size of a postage stamp. Without further ado I put my things on the upper bunk, in two minds about pissing in the corners to mark out my territory. There's absolutely no way I'm going to sleep on that floor. Last come, last served, Pottsy.

'So you're the police officer?' It's said in unmistakable Dutch. Standing behind me in the doorway is a blond, bearded guy in blue coveralls with clogs on his feet and a pencil behind his ears. My quintessentially Dutch room-mate. Add a windmill and a bunch of tulips and the picture would be complete. I can't tell from his voice whether the remark was nasty or meant to be funny.

'Yup,' I sigh. 'Shall I come and file daily reports to assure you that I'm not an undercover agent? I thought I'd proven my credentials last year. Or are you going to be on my back the whole trip to check whether I'm dispatching carrier pigeons to the Dutch security services?'

Wietse stammers, aware that he's got our relationship off to a bad start. 'I… um… well, you see… I've had a lot of unpleasant experiences with the police.'

'But not with me, right?'

'No, but you guys are usually all the same.'

'You guys?' With inane remarks like that I'm afraid it's going to be a very long campaign. 'Why the Dutch clogs?' I quickly add to change the subject. Wietse loosens up instantly.

'I wear them everywhere I go. They're proper work shoes. Made them myself,' he tells me, beaming with pride. Then the clog maker launches into an unsolicited lecture on woodcutting that moves seamlessly into a summary about his life on board. He's been living on the *Steve Irwin* for months, having joined as the ship's carpenter. He's a violin maker by trade. Although not a particularly interesting story, anything is better than an irritating discussion about my police past, which I'm actually proud of to this day.

While we're catching up on Dutch news, Wietse eases up more and more. He enjoys being able to speak his mother tongue again. After 15 minutes of chitchat, he's off with the words that there's still an awful lot to be done. Right now his to-do list is topped by 'the drawers in the mess'.

Wietse and I will get along fine, I think to myself. He's not a bad guy. Back in the day, I used to throw guys like him in a cell whenever a demo got out of hand. Now we'll be spending months in the same room. It's funny how things go.

14

SEA SHEPHERD SAMURAI

Loyalty, determination, obedience, commitment, militancy and a capacity for dealing with stress are the ideal qualities of a Sea Shepherd crew member. They're also the attributes of a Japanese samurai. To underline these similarities, Captain Watson decided to name this year's Antarctica campaign Operation Miyamoto Musashi, after the most illustrious warrior in Japanese history.

The writer of the masterwork on strategy, *The Book of the Five Rings*, a war veteran at the age of sixteen, renowned for his martial arts skills and a master swordsman; what better candidate to lend our campaign a Japanese touch? Obviously Watson chose it to draw attention to the illegal hunt and to provoke a response from the Japanese government. None was forthcoming. The government merely announced it would be spending millions on extra security measures.

And yet the campaign name isn't just a provocation. Musashi's philosophy was that pen and sword are equal. If you want to be victorious, you have to fight. But you also have to win the hearts of your opponent through communication and education. This is a message that Sea Shepherd applauds. With a new season of *Whale Wars*, we'll be trying to convince the world that the cruel practice of whaling ought to be outlawed once and for all.

Like samurai, we're lined up on the bow of the *Steve Irwin*. Well, I say lined up, but in fact our company of shorts, frayed and faded T-shirts and smudged faces is scattered all over the prow. Every now and then a crew member pokes another in the side, so the concentration goes, everyone's in titters and the now irritable group photographer on the quay is back to square one.

In front of the bow, on the quay, the skipper poses with actress Daryl Hannah. She's a good friend of Watson's and has flown over from the States to give the campaign a PR boost. It's doing the trick. The press has turned up in droves today to tease quotes out of the Hollywood star and take photos. They're all jostling with each other for one final shot before the *Steve Irwin* takes to the seas.

But the actress isn't the only crowd puller. In the past year, Sea Shepherd itself has gained in popularity, mainly thanks to the success of the Animal Planet series *Whale Wars*. The programme actually broke viewing records in the United States in its first year. The final episode even attracted more than a million viewers, an unprecedented figure for the channel.

The production company, Lizard Trading, is keen to equal this surprise success, which means that on this trip we've twice as many cameramen, cameras and bits of sound equipment on board. And in addition to walking and talking camera operators, there'll be hidden cameras and microphones on the *Steve Irwin* this year. The producer doesn't want to miss a single shot. It means that our privacy, which was severely compromised to begin with, will be gone altogether. There's no filming without permission in the cabins, but otherwise we'll have cameras in our faces 24 hours a day.

Once all the black Pelican cases with the camera team's electronic equipment have been hauled on board, we're ready to cast off. The crew is itching to swap the murderous heat of the Brisbane River for a cool ocean breeze.

Captain Watson signals that the mooring lines can be taken off the bollards. Under the watchful eye of bosun Daniel, they're hurriedly pulled in by the nervous rookies heading out on their first campaign. The ship's horn blasts a final goodbye to the waving supporters on the quay. Slowly, the *Steve Irwin* navigates the muddy waters of the Brisbane and sets sail for Newcastle, where we can get the cheapest fuel.

The campaign gets underway with 48 crew members: 33 men and 15 women. Of these, 23 are veterans, while 25 are setting out on their first campaign. With 14 people, the Australians are in the majority, with the rest made up of Americans, New Zealanders, Swedes, Germans, Dutch, Hungarians, South Africans and one Bermudan.

And before I forget: we almost had a stowaway. The man in question was an old friend of Watson's, from the days when smoking weed was all the rage. Since he seemed to live in a world of his own, we all thought Rod was permanently stoned. In the end, the errant mariner wasn't allowed to come along. He begged to differ. So when the first mate checked to see if the rebel was on the quay, the sexagenarian was missing. Just before we set off, the ship was searched. The stowaway was hiding in the shower cubicles in the forward part of the ship. Rod ended up waving us goodbye from the quay, with drooping shoulders and obvious reluctance.

After a brief stop in Newcastle we sail on to Hobart for our final stopover. While crossing the Bass Strait the captain tests the propeller pitch at 75 per cent capacity, which is about the maximum. It will allow the *Steve Irwin* to reach a speed of 15 knots, enough to keep up with the factory ship *Nisshin Maru*.

In Hobart, Tasmania, the ship takes in another 30,000 litres of diesel, bringing the total to 200,000 tonnes. The water tanks are topped up to 60,000 litres. One thing we don't have on board is a watermaker to make seawater drinkable. The water in the tanks is for showering, washing and cooking food. When it's gone, we'll have to return to port. To avoid this, tight restrictions on water use apply. The lousiest one is the shower rule: one three-minute shower every three days. No exceptions. If you want a good lather-up, you can choose not to shower for six days and then indulge for six minutes. Another option is to swap toilet cleaning duty with someone for three extra minutes.

We spend two days in Hobart. As in all the other Australian port cities Sea Shepherd calls at, we receive a lot of support from the local population. Repairs and installations are done free of charge, donations are left by the gangplank and every day a bunch of volunteers turn up to do odd jobs or drive the crew around town for errands. There's a feeling among the Australians that the whaling is taking place in their back garden, since much of it is done in Australia's Exclusive Economic Zone (EEZ) in Antarctica. Australia's High Court recently ruled cetacean hunting illegal under the Environment Protection and Biodiversity Conservation Act 1999. And although Watson keeps bending politicians' ears, the judgement has so far failed to yield any government action. And it probably comes as no surprise that Japan has completely ignored the ruling as well.

Opinion polls in the Australian papers suggest that the public is clamouring for a patrol ship in the South Pole region. Politicians, however, are more concerned with protecting trade interests. This kind of political expediency is something Sea Shepherd will not condone. In fact it's now time for us to put away our pens and draw our swords. What else can we do now that the illegal whaling fleet is approaching Antarctica? At 17.40 hours on 10 December 2008 the *Steve Irwin* leaves port for Operation Musashi.

15

FIRE ON BOARD?

Position: 59° 47' S, 138° 37' E.

Since passing the 50th parallel south, our flagship has been taking a terrible beating. Towering waves are pounding the vessel into submission. Each wave lifts the *Steve Irwin* several metres, followed by a free fall lasting several seconds. When the bow slams back down on the water, the vibrations can be felt throughout the ship. Two days ago, bosun Daniel warned us that a violent storm was coming and ordered all the hatches and porthole covers to be screwed shut to prevent seawater from seeping in and to keep the portholes intact. A sensible decision, because right now it's far too dangerous to venture outside.

In the evening, the view from the bridge is terrifying: the *Steve Irwin* is surrounded by a swirling mass of black water. Waves reaching peaks of more than 10 metres race across the ocean, where the wind is free to vent its anger. It's pitch-dark in the pilothouse, with only the faint glow of a couple of computer screens illuminating the gloomy space. Nobody says much, as the quartermasters peer through the windows, mesmerised by the formidable force of nature. The ship is on autopilot, but the helmsman is ready to intervene in case something goes wrong.

A steering error can be fatal. The ship is regularly taking 40-degree rolls. According to the experienced sailors, this isn't a problem for the *Steve Irwin*. The less experienced sailors, myself included, are doubtful. Nautical charts, paper, pens, tea cups, just about everything that's not fastened down goes flying through the bridge if there's no hand holding on to it. Each roll seems to send a whirlwind through the pilothouse.

Those with sea legs lean into the waves so as not to fall over. Those who've had enough go to the mess, one of the ship's lowest and most stable areas. In the mess the crew is trying to take its mind off things by playing games, reading or watching TV. We're all dreading a rogue wave, a wave – perhaps twice as high as the waves currently battering our ship – that appears out of nowhere and can be a threat even to large ocean steamers such as oil tankers. So imagine the damage it could inflict on this tiny black cork floating in this gigantic, Antarctic bathtub.

Despite the heavy weather outside, the atmosphere inside the mess is chilled. Wietse is carving a small whale out of a piece of wood, probably for Emily Hunter, whom he fancies. On-board romances are not a good idea, as they distract from the mission, but they're inevitable as soon as you confine a group of men and women on a ship. The budding romances are usually kept secret until we're back on dry land and the pent-up hormones can finally be released.

Emily is lying stretched across the sofa in the mess. Her face has a greyish-green tinge, since she's one of the few still affected by seasickness. Wietse can't make his move just yet.

Molly's busy tuning the guitar that's always in a corner of the mess. That thing has been out of tune for as long as anyone can remember. And every year there'll be someone trying to tune it.

Andy's balancing two full mugs of ginger tea as he comes out of the galley when the ship's rolling sideways. He only just manages to keep the tea inside. Andy hands one mug to Molly and snuggles up to her.

Arne and I are playing a game of Scopa, an Italian card game the German has brought along. He's on a winning streak and I suspect he may be interpreting the rules in his own favour. Arne denies this. A German and a Dutchman playing a game together, that's asking for trouble.

The evening meal is followed by a TV series. The captain gets to choose. You can suggest something else if you want, but his word is law. Luckily we tend to watch epics featuring heroes and fierce battles. So tonight is not the first time Watson and I lay claim to two easy chairs and park them right in front of the television. The Canadian has a superb memory and accompanies each battle with a detailed commentary; the facts about various wars and historical figures hurtle by just as fast as the English subtitles on the screen. The captain jokes that the Dutch are a foolish people, plugging a dyke with their fingers (the story of Hans Brinker) and spending millions on tulip bulbs in the seventeenth century. All I do is brag about the Golden Age, when 'we' ruled the waves.

The storm hasn't died down yet. Every time a wave smashes hard against the hull, everybody in the mess looks up. The dilated, startled eyes betray what few are prepared to admit: this storm is pretty serious and seemingly never-ending.

One of the engineers has come to get a coffee from the galley. His face is covered in black smudges and his worried frown speaks volumes. Having spent days scaling mountains of water, the engines of this old ship are struggling to cope. As quickly as he appeared, the hard worker scuttles off again, back to the engine room. I can't even begin to express my admiration for the engineers, always hidden away, deep down, in the dark, growling bowels of the ship.

On the way to my cabin, I bump into Daniel who's moving slowly along the wall panelling. He looks worried.

'You smell that?' he asks.

I hadn't noticed the unpleasant smell before. 'Smells like fire.'

'Exactly.'

One of the engineers comes running out of the engine room, where the smell has also penetrated. 'It's not us,' he says immediately, which is a relief. The smell of smoke quickly spreads through the corridors, and yet nobody can figure out where it's coming from. Command is informed and soon everybody who's awake is trying to locate the source of the fire.

There's no panic just yet, but now that even the chief engineer has been woken up I know the situation is alarming. If a fire breaks out on our ship and it's not immediately brought under control, the *Steve Irwin* will turn into a floating inferno in no time. And in this weather it's not safe to launch the lifeboats. I'm not the only one to realise this. Despite the absence of fire, the thought alone is enough to see normally tough-looking faces take on decidedly anxious expressions.

Everyone's joined the search now. There's a cloud of smoke in the narrow corridors, a mere film, but definitely visible. The chief engineer is patting each wall with the flat of his hand to see if it's warm. Who knows, maybe the fire has broken out inside the partitions, where the electrical wiring is. In that case, the fire will spread unseen.

While I'm searching, I quickly slip into my cabin to swap my Teva sandals for waterproof shoes and to put some warm clothes on. If this is more than just a scare and we're ordered to abandon ship, I want to be dressed appropriately.

The fire still hasn't been located. Captain Watson is now walking up and down the corridors, sniffing and touching the walls. 'Has anyone had a look outside?' he asks a small group of crew members standing by the exit to the afterdeck. They all stare at the skipper. How could there possibly be a fire outside? With this mad gale blowing, wind and rain battering the deck and huge waves washing over the ship?

'No,' is the collective response.

Watson opens the door to the afterdeck. The storm yanks at the heavy wooden door. He steps outside and I follow. We're standing there with the wind tugging at us and the waves washing over the deck, but there's nothing to be seen.

We hold on tight to the railing as we shuffle to starboard side. I'm trying to keep three points of contact so as not to lose my balance. No sooner have I stuck my head round the corner than I spot a column of orange smoke getting whipped away by the wind; some disappears inside through an air vent, while the rest is swallowed up by the darkness. The smoke is flaring up from a smoke signal attached to a lifebuoy. A huge wave knocked the buoy off the bridge wing, triggering the smoke signal.

'Give me your knife,' the soaking wet captain yells above the howling wind. He knows I'm carrying a knife, like all sailors should. I hand Watson my Spider and with the razor-sharp serrated blade he cuts the smoke signal off the buoy. The flare is thrown overboard, the buoy is taken inside. Just before we re-enter, an icy wave crashes over us. Soaked to the skin, but grinning broadly, we're back in the corridor.

'It was the lifebuoy,' the captain says matter-of-factly. He walks straight through to his quarters, as if nothing unusual has happened. I stay behind, dripping wet and amazed to think that on a ship any carefree moment can turn treacherous in seconds. And that the paralysing thought of peril may be a bigger danger than the threat itself.

16

ICE, ICE EVERYWHERE

Position: 65° 42' S, 141° 13' E.

'Great God, this is an awful place!'
Explorer Robert Falcon Scott (1868–1912) on Antarctica

A couple of days ago we came across our first harpoon ship. It resulted in my first rubber boat action. Unfortunately it didn't pan out too well: we were hit by bad weather and barely made it back to the *Steve Irwin*. The perilous undertaking left Molly with a big bump on her chin, while the rest of us had a lucky escape.

Meanwhile the *Steve Irwin* is setting course for the *Nisshin Maru*'s last known location. Molly's swelling is going down quickly; it's only a matter of days until she's fully recovered. She's her usual cheery self, stomping around the ship with a big smile on her face. Her fiancé, Andy, on the other hand is still in a huff about the decision to launch the dinghy in that crazy weather. He reckons bosun Daniel should have refused, quite simply because it was irresponsible. And he's hacked off with himself. He could have said no. So could I. But who'd be the first to do so? If you're the only one to speak up, you'll be known as a coward for the remainder of the trip. If others back you up, you'll be the sensible one. It was a decision neither of us was prepared to take in the face of peer pressure. The longing for action prevailed.

The storm that overtook us still hasn't died down. Strong winds blow large slabs of drift ice up from the continent and into our path. In this bad weather it's getting harder and harder to avoid the growlers and ice floes. Our speed is slowing steadily.

The *Steve Irwin* has no ice class; a large piece of ice is all it would take to sink us. And now that thick blankets of fog are descending on the ship as well, extreme caution is called for. The command dispatches me to the bow in a bright orange Mustang suit to indicate the approach of any dangerous growlers. I start flapping my arms about like a traffic controller until we're surrounded by so much ice that I look as if I'm about to take off. Our ship slows to just a few knots and squeezes past the chunks of ice all around us.

An enormous tabular iceberg appears on the radar. These ice floes, kilometres long and dozens of metres high, break off from the Antarctic continent and drift slowly north until, after years of wandering, they've melted. A large expanse of water has opened up behind this gigantic windbreak. Watson decides to sit out the bad weather in the lee of the iceberg. We'll wait here until the wind turns, slowly circling in the open water. But that night, the wind direction changes to north-west. The circles get smaller as the ice creeps up on us and completely encloses the *Steve Irwin*.

Antarctica is cutting us down to size. Wind and ice rule this no-man's-land, not man. We're stuck. The landscape is full of ice, as far as the eye can see. Age-old floes, pale blue and densely packed, alternate with new sea ice compressed into a firm pack. Here and there some narrow channels open up among the drift ice, but the chance of us getting through in one piece is minute. The *Steve Irwin* is shifting back and forth to keep the space around the propeller and the rudder free of ice.

Captain Watson, the one in ultimate command, has taken over the helm and is now moving the ship forwards at a couple of knots. In order to spare the ship's fragile skin as much as possible, the skipper sails head-on into the growlers that block our way to a wider channel. He doesn't always pull it off; every so often growlers scrape past the hull, leaving traces of red paint from the bottom of the ship on the snow-white ice. Any moment now one of these ice cliffs might rip our bow and prove fatal.

Fear is taking hold of the ship. The crew is talking nervously, sometimes in whispers, about wanting to be home. Some even grumble that we should never have ended up in the ice, but should have sought out open sea. We all have our opinions, but none of them matter. It's up to the captain to decide how to proceed. He has many years' experience sailing through ice. That's the message with which the officers try to reassure us. Still, the nightmare scenario in which the ship is ripped open and sinks several kilometres to the bottom of the ocean keeps haunting most of us. Even the reassurance that some compartments can be sealed doesn't do the trick. We try to put a brave face on it, but we can't help but be afraid.

Down in our cabin, Wietse, Pottsy and I make sure that our emergency kits and survival suits are ready in case we spring a leak. Every time an ice floe scrapes past the hull, we hear a loud creaking noise in our room. No place on the ship offers a respite from the shrill and terrifying scraping noise.

Watson is trying to force his way through the thickening ice. But then the *Steve Irwin* grinds to a halt against a large floe; the ship isn't powerful enough to push the massive ice sheet aside. Bosun Daniel checks the inside of the fo'c'sle, right behind the wall of the bow. Two seconds later he's back again, waving both arms to tell the bridge to stop at once. He reckons the ice is too thick. Every time we ram it, the ship's steel plating is pushed several centimetres inwards. It's only a matter of time before the thin wall and the girders cave in and the fo'c'sle floods.

The ship's carpenter is summoned to the fo'c'sle at once. Time's breathing down Wietse's neck because after the umpteenth collision, the ship's plating is so badly dented the paint is coming off on the inside. He's knocking together wedges as fast as he can, shivers running down his spine. Next, Arne and Simon shore up the transverse frames as best as they can to take pressure off the skin. Cameraman John Manns films the brave deckies' every move. Another loud bang.

John puts his camera down on a tangle of ropes, lens aimed at the deckhands' tense faces, and calls it quits: 'This is where my commitment ends.' The camera keeps rolling, while the cameraman scoots up the ladder. Back on deck he tells us that this is insane before he's off to get his survival suit. Daniel peers down the hole leading to the fo'c'sle: 'Are you OK down there, guys?'

'For now, yes,' Simon replies.

Another loud thud and harsh scraping.

'Oh shit,' we hear from down below, followed by a lengthy pause. 'No, really, it's fine, why don't you join us?' Simon yells irritably.

Nobody in their right mind would willingly accept that invitation.

The search for open water continues. Every now and then a narrow channel opens up and the *Steve Irwin* pushes a couple of metres ahead. This is followed by periods in which we don't move an inch. During one of the rare moments we're allowed to rest, I withdraw to my cabin. Whenever an ice floe scrapes past, I'm paralysed with fear.

I don't want to be here anymore.

Don't be stupid. If there's a breach we'll repair it. A loud thud.

I really don't fancy the prospect of having to survive in Antarctica.

All's quiet again.

The captain has been navigating through ice for years. He'll get us out of here.

Another growler scrapes across the hull.

Shut up, the ship's going down.

It'll be fine. If the worst comes to the worst, they'll send a rescue plane.

An ice floe rolls under the hull and on to the rear, leaving the steel shuddering and screeching.

We're dying.

Reason and emotion are doing battle in my head. But whoever I proclaim the winner, the situation itself won't change. We can't expect help as the nearest source is at least 2,500 sea miles away. My fate is in the hands of the people on the bridge. This sobering conclusion calms me down. Acquiescence takes the place of uncertainty. I lie down on my bed and close my eyes: there's someone else whose help we can call on. It may have been 15 years, but after the many storms, my life-threatening stunt in the rubber boat and now the battering ice, this may be a good moment to restore contact:

'God, we're here to save whales. Your creatures. And we could do with a bit of help. I know we're a bunch of amateurs and pretty clumsy at times, but we're doing our best. I'm sure You can see that. I don't want to be a hypocrite, but I do want to get the hell out of here. I won't make empty promises, but if You help us, then…'

Pottsy flings the door open and switches the light on.

'Were you jerking off?'

'Um, no, having a rest.'

'Yeah, sure, just clean up after yourself, will you? And when you're done, come to the deck. We're launching a rubber boat to push away the ice.'

'Amen.'

Lo and behold, our nerve-racking times are coming to an end. Word on the bridge is that the wind has turned. More and more channels are emerging among the ice floes. Our bow is squeezing through the cracks, metre by metre. It's agonisingly slow, but at least we're moving. The Delta is sailing behind the *Steve Irwin* to keep the propeller free of ice. The bow is still sighing and creaking every time we collide with the ice, but because it's now less tightly packed, we manage to carefully nudge aside the floes. The edge of the ice is in sight.

With open water on the horizon, the mood turns like a leaf on a tree. Suddenly the crew is enjoying the beautiful scenery. People are pointing to icebergs which have been sculpted into fairy-tale castles by the wind. A stray Adélie penguin hurriedly dives into the water when the steel colossus chugs past and a leopard seal growls in the distance. The scenery is breathtaking. The wondrous white world of the South Pole had been pounding us like a battering-ram, and for a while we were arch enemies, but now all is forgiven.

The captain heads towards open water at a couple of knots per hour. Now that we're nearly free of the ice, the wind sweeps freely across the water's surface. The surge lifts enormous growlers from the trough to the top of the wild billows. A chunk could knock a hole the size of a car into our hull. The ice is invisible in a trough. The captain won't let go of the helm until he's manoeuvred the *Steve Irwin* out of this minefield, around the passing growlers. Watson makes it look easy, but his frown suggests the utmost concentration.

Hours of ploughing later and we're surrounded only by gigantic tabular icebergs. The pack ice is gone and the wind has died down. The ice has set us back days, but hasn't defeated us. Even the captain, who's been sailing the Seven Seas his whole life, agreed afterwards that this was one of the diciest moments in his life at sea.

Simon and Arne climb out of the fo'c'sle. They did a job nobody else was prepared to do. In the event of a breach, they would have been the first to brave the ice water gushing in. The deckies were guarding the fortress at its most vulnerable point. But Simon is quite matter-of-fact as he sums up his heroic exploits: 'Life as a deckhand: one minute you're saving the ship from sinking, the next minute you're cleaning toilets.'

17

MAN OVERBOARD

For days now we've been tailing the *Nisshin Maru*. It's ahead of us somewhere, but every day we don't lay eyes on it, the death squad seems further away than ever. We did come across another vessel: the *Spirit of Endeavour*, a cruise ship no less. For its passengers, the encounter was an added bonus on their tour of Antarctica. For us a dampener. But since Sea Shepherd relies on donors, the captain decided to make the most of the situation and offer the tourists a snapshot.

Our helicopter took off for a flying pose with the *Steve Irwin* in all its glory in the background. Hundreds of cameras were flashing non-stop to capture an image of the activists. The situation had a surreal quality to it, as if you're running after a burglar and suddenly stop to have your picture taken with a passer-by. Hopefully the travellers will donate a bit of cash and generate some publicity for us. After the commercial break, the captain of the *Endeavour* told us that he hadn't passed the whaling fleet and wished us luck.

On Boxing Day we're back on track. We pass the *Kaiko Maru*, a spotter ship. This vessel makes its way across the ocean very, very slowly, looking for pods of whales and then relaying their location to the harpoon throwers. Their reprehensible job is rewarded with a load of butyric acid. The *Kaiko* thinks it best to flee, but Watson decides not to give chase because we need to save fuel if we want to catch up with the *Nisshin*.

New Year's Eve follows and the fleet is still sailing somewhere far beyond the horizon, out of reach. We're reflecting on the campaign with mixed feelings. 2009 dawns. Party time under normal circumstances, but today we're celebrating modestly. A bottle of wine is passed round and the captain sets off a flare. For a while its red, flickering light hangs lonely and forlorn in the twilit sky. Until we track down the hunters we have nothing to celebrate. One of the quartermasters stuffs our wishes into an empty wine bottle and chucks it into the sea. No prizes for guessing what everyone is wishing for.

It's another five days before an unfortunate event lends us an advantage. Last night a crew member on one of the harpoon ships went overboard. A slippery deck, a treacherous wave or simply a moment of inattention and the sea swallows you up. If only he had heard our second mate's lecture about pissing on a boat. Of course it's highly unlikely that the whaler will be found alive, but the fleet nonetheless transmits a distress signal.

We decide to approach the fleet to assist with the search. Sea Shepherd is here to save whales, but not at the expense of the most important maritime law: a ship in trouble must be helped. Even if it's a whaler.

Bright searchlights sweep the water's surface. Via the radio, Sea Shepherd offers to deploy its rubber boats and helicopter. The Japanese captain declines the offer outright: 'We will not ask you to help out due to the fact that you are environmental terrorists.'

We try to make contact again. No response. Suit yourself. We follow at an appropriate distance and promise to look out for the man who's gone overboard. Now that we're close to the whalers, they'll be searching for days, or pretending to, so we don't obstruct the hunt. Our captain reckons it's better to head back to Hobart to refuel before the whalers stop their rescue efforts and resume the hunt and we're without fuel. We wish the Japanese crew good luck and promise to be back soon.

The moment we leave the whaling convoy, a harpoon ship creeps up on us. Watson asks if this manoeuvre is part of the search and rescue. No response. If the *Yushin Maru* keeps following us, we'll launch the rubber boats, our skipper warns. No change. We launch the RIBs.

In a jiffy both rubber boats are rushing after the harpoon ship. We've warned the ship this chase has nothing to do with the search and rescue effort anymore. Our prop fouler is in the Gemini, ready for action. If we manage to get closer, that prop fouler will be hurled underneath. With a bit of luck we'll finally eliminate a hunter.

The harpoon ship takes off, bouncing across the waves. The distance we have to bridge is getting longer and longer. Although the Gemini can do 40 knots, we have to slow down on the crests so as not to propel ourselves out of the boat. Simon can't do more than 15 knots. Again, we're forced to abort a chase. We carry on hounding the vessel until it's far enough away for the *Steve Irwin* to remain out of radar range. But then, bitterly disappointed, we return to our mother ship. Will we ever get close to these super-fast and manoeuvrable harpoon ships? We keep trying, but we're beginning to have some misgivings.

The crew is in a sombre mood. The first part of the campaign was not without setbacks: failed boat launches, a storm, ice and a fruitless search. We find solace in the thought that, while they're running away from us, they're not catching any whales. But that's by no means certain.

In the port of Hobart, we long to be back at sea. We want to finish the job. Wietse, my room-mate, has to leave the ship due to other commitments. We got off to a bad start, but we say goodbye with a big hug. The battle at sea, risking your life together: it creates a bond for life. There was plenty we disagreed about, but our shared passion, protecting whales, eclipsed any differences of opinion. Pouring our hearts out when things got tough, pondering the meaning of life into the early hours and covering each other's backs on the bow as a hunter approached: all these moments with my room-mate have culminated in a friendship that will last forever.*

One final stop before we set off again. The Mission to Seafarers, a kind of church-sponsored seamen's pub, contains a small chapel. The entrance boasts a statue of the Virgin Mary surrounded by candles and flowers. Next to it are portraits of a number of patron saints. I light a candle.

Sailing has a strange effect on you. It gives you faith, or superstition, whatever you want to call it. If we weather a storm it's because an albatross didn't land on the ship. A good launch is put down to the socks I'm wearing that day. The passage of a pod of whales is a gift from Mother Nature while we have Neptune to thank for a beautiful day, granting us safe conduct. You start looking for explanations for all the exciting, strange, dangerous and beautiful things that cross your path. It's easier to ascribe them to higher powers than to logic – it's a survival mechanism for the lowly seaman on the mighty ocean.

The body of the Japanese seaman was never found. The sea is cruel.

---

* In the summer of 2010 Wietse founded The Black Fish. This international marine conservation organisation fights the industrial overfishing of our ocean – www.theblackfish.org

18

TORA, TORA, HUH?

Position: 67° 34' S, 174° 36' W.

On 2 February 2009 we stumble upon the entire whaling fleet. Perhaps the Japanese guard had slipped and they didn't have anyone manning the radar or maybe they weren't expecting us back so soon. What we owe this to I don't know, but it's certainly a sweet surprise.

Now that we've got the *Nisshin Maru* and the harpoon ships in our sights, we hoist our banners: the flags of the United Nations (because we uphold the regulations of the World Charter for Nature), the Five Nations (a Native American flag presented to us by the Iroquois), Operation Musashi, the Australian Aboriginals, the Netherlands (where the ship is registered) and Sea Shepherd. All six fly proudly on their flagpoles.

But this year the rancid butter will be hurled from the rubber boats. After our previous campaign we received a lot of criticism from the Dutch authorities. Needless to say, one of their grievances was the fact that we were throwing from our ship. So as not to blow our credit we'll take a different tack this year. It will be tricky, but not impossible.

As soon as the weather permits, the helicopter pilot takes off to circle above the factory ship. To his surprise, he notices some serious countermeasures on board the whaling vessel. 'The days of them hiding inside their cabins are over,' Chris sums it up. 'They're all out on deck, ready for battle. The flensing deck is cordoned off with a big black net. It's going to be tricky to throw anything over. The good news is that I haven't spotted any coastguards, and they're not cutting up any whales right now.' The Japanese police have stayed at home, which suggests that the international uproar did have an effect.

When he comes back from the bridge, Daniel relays the orders to us and then the Delta is off to throw butyric acid on the *Nisshin*'s deck. Team Gemini is supposed to stop the *Yushin Maru 3* with the prop fouler. The prop fouler's blue Kevlar cables are indestructible, or so we've been told by its makers. We roll it out one last time on deck before squeezing it into the green wheelie bin that's strapped down in the back of the Gemini. We also load a pile of butyric acid.

The weather is pretty calm, and judging by the deckies' faces we're all raring to go. Let the battle commence, or as first officer Hammarstedt tells us on a daily basis, usually in vain, but now justifiably: 'The whaling ends today.'

The 7-metre Gemini is packed, and sets off in pursuit with seven crew members on board. We make a quick dash for the *Yushin Maru 3*, and within minutes we've caught up. Simon, our driver, stares straight ahead, because the water is littered with treacherous ice floes. Our chopper hovers above the harpoon ship, with the pilot advising us over the radio about any open water so we can cross in front of the harpoon ship's bow.

I contact the *Steve Irwin* on the VHF radio: 'Bridge, this is the Gemini. We're at the target, ready for your orders.'

'Tora, tora, tora.' (Japanese code for charge and attack.)

'We copy, tora, tora, tora.'

We all look at the bosun with question marks in our eyes.

'Uh… that's the code phrase for throwing butyric acid.'

'Oh, OK.' Daniel and I swap places. He'll navigate while I throw.

Chris comes blaring over the radio. 'Gemini, there's a stretch of open water ahead. Coming up in about 30 seconds, I estimate.'

'Thanks Chris.' Simon turns to starboard and at 30 knots zips towards the bow of the harpoon ship. I've taken off my thick winter gloves and am now just wearing thin, plastic washing-up gloves for a better grip on the bottles of butyric acid. Finally, after the endless wait, I'm face to face with one of the monstrous harpoon vessels. We have just one goal: to hit the harpoon and stink the thing up so badly no Japanese will venture out on deck.

The Gemini cuts across the bow of the *Yushin Maru*. Jets of water from the tiny water cannon at the front graze our small boat. It's a streak of piss compared to the immense water cannons on the *Nisshin Maru*.

'Ready?' the bosun yells.

A nod and a thumbs-up are all it takes.

'You only get one shot, do not miss the chance to blow,' I recite in my head.

Simon accelerates and the Gemini cuts sharply across the front of the bow. The harpooner is doing everything it can to get away, but this time we're too fast for them. My bottle of butyric acid flies towards the harpoon and bursts on top of the device. A direct hit. The photographer takes a quick shot, which will make it into the papers later. As Simon zigzags in front of the bow, we throw bottle after bottle onto the prow. The harpoon ship gives off a terrible stench. We did it! At last, a successful action!

'Bridge, this is the Gemini, over.'

'Go ahead, Gemini.'

'We did it. We delivered the rancid butter.'

'Rancid butter? But what about tora, tora, tora?'

Taken aback, Daniel stammers over the radio: 'Th-th-that was the butter, right?'

'No, you idiot.' It's Peter who's relaying the messages, but I can tell from his voice that he's repeating the words of a furious captain.

'You were supposed to foul the prop. Now the element of surprise is gone. Why can't you do as you're told?'

'Roger, over.'

The bosun has been ticked off, but none of us in the rubber boat gives a damn. We kicked the harpoon ship's ass and now we'll just as happily foul its prop. If we pull it off, we'll eliminate a harpoon ship today. We're quite confident we can do it with our 'indestructible' prop fouler.

The helicopter is still in the air. A nice long stretch of open water is coming up ahead. The wheelie bin is opened. Daniel and I swap places again in the crowded rubber boat, because he's launching the prop fouler from the back.

It's all down to timing now. Simon keeps a close eye on the water in front of us. A single chunk of ice could do serious damage to our propeller.

The Gemini is sailing parallel to the *Yushin* before it tears across the front in a wide arc. The bosun throws one end of the prop fouler into the water. As soon as it hits the water, the rest is yanked out of the wheelie bin, forming a long, floating line on the water surface. We all hold our breath as the harpoon ship approaches. A miss! The Japanese ship pulls abruptly to port and just manages to avoid the prop fouler.

'Damn! Too early,' Daniel yells. 'Quick, let's go and retrieve it.'

Simon turns the Gemini around. The *Yushin Maru* takes advantage by speeding off.

The water we're in is clear blue, with chunks of pristine white drift ice bobbing around and doubling as a diving board for the coy penguins. A gorgeous panorama we would enjoy immensely if it weren't for the fact that the makers of the prop fouler had opted to use the colour blue for the line and white for the floats. The rope is virtually invisible in this landscape, and it takes us more than 20 minutes to spot it around an ice floe.

We all set about tugging the heavy rope back on board, but the last bit is caught around a protruding piece of ice. We can't get to it by boat because of an ice foot just below the surface.

'Do you reckon it will hold me?' thrower Richard wonders.

Before we have a chance to respond, he steps onto the ice floe. Brittle pieces of ice crumble off and the floe sinks a little deeper now that it's supporting Richard's weight. One wrong move and he'll find himself in the −1.5 degree Antarctic water. With the *Steve Irwin* 7 sea miles away, there's a very real chance our daredevil will pay for his stunt with fatal hypothermia.

'You're out of your mind,' we exclaim in unison. On his knees, the stuntman shuffles towards the tip where the rope is wedged tight. Balancing on one arm and both legs, he reaches for the rope with his other arm and yanks it free. He's done it! As the prop fouler slips off, the ice floe wobbles. Richard crawls back to the Gemini and jumps on board. He's triumphant: 'I've always wanted to set foot on Antarctica. And now I have.'

Unfortunately, the *Yushin Maru 3* has disappeared from sight. Captain Watson asks us to assist the Delta with the *Nisshin Maru*. We race towards the 130-metre abattoir and join the other rubber boat.

'We can't get those bottles on deck,' the Delta crew tell us. 'It's like trying to throw a bottle onto the Empire State Building.'

'Maybe we can do it via the slipway,' Daniel suggests.

'You're joking, have you seen those water cannons?'

'It's worth a try.'

Simon steers the Gemini towards the factory ship's wake. Two criss-crossing water cannons, which are pumping up icy seawater and directing high-pressure jets at our boat, block the access to the slipway. The jets are at least 20 centimetres wide. One of the Japanese crew operates the cannons from a small cabin just left above the slipway. Where the jets zigzag in front of the slipway they leave a narrow zone in the middle that seems to be free of water. Our bosun tells the driver to sail straight down the middle. The Gemini approaches the slipway at high speed, but nonetheless hits an enormous wall of water. The brutal jets spurting across our rubber boat put me in mind of a swirling car wash. I can't see a thing and I'm gasping for breath. Those on board who fail to duck in time are walloped hard. Simon immediately shifts into reverse.

Richard is lying upside-down against the middle console, coughing the water out of his lungs. Our photographer has been shot back along the full length of the boat and then nearly tumbled overboard beside the outboard motors. The Animal Planet cameraman is groaning in the back seat. The others just had a real fright.

'What's up?' I ask.

'Got hit in the face. I was filming, so I didn't see that jet coming.'

'Let's see.' He lifts his head and squints at me. Blood is pouring from his nose, but worse, from his right eye as well. It's unclear whether there's a tear under his eye or whether the blood is trickling from his eye socket, but it's certainly not looking good. The cameraman needs urgent assistance.

'Return to the ship, Simon, he needs to see the doctor.'

'Aye, aye.'

After we drop the cameraman off at the rope ladder, take a new one on board and replace two busted cameras, the command asks if we could have another go at prop fouling the harpoon ship. Even though we've been on the water for several hours, we're soaking wet and the cold is starting to seep through our clothes, we refuse to call it a day. The crew members wolf down energy bars, drink some water and then race straight back to the whaler.

Simon steers the Gemini around the small bundles of ice we encounter. I trust him implicitly. It's as if we're riding a bike, such is his control of the rubber boat. And although this is our first Antarctica campaign together, we're working like a seasoned team. It doesn't take us long to find the *Yushin Maru 3.*

'Here we go again, guys,' our bosun yells in high spirits. We open the lid of the wheelie bin and wait for a sign from the chopper pilot. The Japanese crew run around the deck, with the odd one giving us the finger or shouting something incomprehensible though undoubtedly offensive.

'Now!' we hear from the helicopter.

Simon doesn't think twice, pulls up to starboard side and heads for the steep bow. I'm at the helm, trying to assist the driver as best as I can.

'Ready?'

'Yes.'

'Hold… hold… hold… now!' When Simon turns left, I yell at Daniel: 'Go… Go… Go!'

The prop fouler slides into the water and now lies right across the front of the harpoon ship. When the *Yushin Maru* sails over the rope it is immediately sucked under.

'It's working, it's working,' the bosun yells excitedly.

The Gemini rushes to the stern. No rope re-emerges. The Kevlar must have wrapped itself around the propeller.

'Bridge, our present is on its way.' Collective whoops of joy over the radio.

'Is the vessel slowing down, Chris?' the second mate is curious to know.

'No, it's still cruising at 16 knots.'

Bye-bye, enthusiasm. If the propeller were really damaged, the ship could never continue. Suddenly, some 15 metres of prop fouler is spat out by the *Yushin*'s rear. The propeller simply cut through the rope.

'God damn it, that bloody thing was supposed to be indestructible,' rages Daniel. 'Absolutely unbreakable.' We'd been assured that the

Australian coastguard had eliminated dozens of ships with this type of prop fouler. It cost more than AUD$20,000, but has been ripped to shreds after our first action.

The disastrous news goes down like a lead balloon on the bridge. We had one chance. Sea Shepherd could only afford one Kevlar prop fouler. We have a couple of homemade ropes on board, but this was our only serious weapon against the harpoon ships. The seven of us risked our lives by lurking in front of that bow and then the whole thing comes to nothing. All that's left is a lousy little bit of prop fouler. Maybe we can try again later, who knows, but none of us has much faith in it.

'Gemini, please return to base,' the bridge orders. 'We found a massive snowstorm on the radar and we don't know how fast it's approaching. The sleet is pelting down over here.' Where we are, the sky is blue with the odd scattered cloud, but they certainly don't look like ominous thunderclouds. It shows, once again, just how dependent we are on our weather maps and instruments.

'Roger. We're on our way.'

'What shall we do, guys? Are we heading straight back or shall we go and say goodbye?'

In unison: 'Say goodbye!'

Our last few bottles of butyric acid fly towards the Japanese hunter. The crew on deck doesn't let us get away with it and they start hurling all kinds of objects at us.

'Take cover,' Richard screams. As we duck we hear things landing in the water around us.

'Tap-tap-tap!' It's the sound of a hailstorm of large nuts, bolts and pieces of lead hitting the rubber boat. When I look up, a gold-coloured bolt hits first my visor and then my face. If it hadn't been for my helmet the bolt would have injured my eye. Simon decides to head back before the situation further escalates.

The *Steve Irwin* is about 8 sea miles away, chasing the *Nisshin Maru* at around 15 knots. We'd better hurry up or we'll drop too far behind. The Gemini appears to be catching up on the mother ship until we hit a maze of sea ice. Whichever way we look, left or right, we can't see a way through. Slowly, very slowly, the driver navigates his way through the jungle of ice, but we keep getting stuck.

Over the VHF radio I'm given the coordinates of the waypoint where the *Steve* is headed. They're drawing ahead of us. The sky is clouding over and not much later the first few snowflakes start to whirl down from the grey mass of cloud. If we're unlucky, visibility will be down to zero and we'll be forced to shelter behind an iceberg. We can't expect help; in this kind of weather our helicopter will remain grounded. And our on-board radar is useless: the screen is completely white.

At this point we've been on the Antarctic water for over 6 hours. The wind has picked up, chilling us to the bone. Now that our adrenaline has worn off, the cold is gaining the upper hand. Daniel, peeing with his Mustang coveralls down around his ankles and shivering with cold, tells us that the warm jet feels heavenly. We share a couple of energy bars to give our bodies a bit more fuel. We keep searching for a passage through, but it takes forever just to cover a couple of metres.

I contact our mother ship to ask them to slow down, because we're not doing more than 3 knots. Only half the message gets through. I can't understand the response. Has the connection been lost? I keep trying, but Simon reckons the whalers are jamming our radio transmissions. Without communication we'll never find our ship. From under the middle console Daniel pulls a yellow Pelican case with the satellite phone. But as soon as he switches the device on, the battery dies. The frost has proven too much for the equipment. It's impossible to make a call.

'All we can do is return to the last known location of the *Steve Irwin*. And hope they'll wait for us,' Simon concludes.

An hour later both our mood and the temperature have dropped to well below freezing. The sleet has turned us into snowmen and the wind lashes any facial skin that's not covered by ski goggles or scarves. Bits of snow are freezing in my sailor's stubble. We're zigzagging through the archipelago of ice, feeling low and freezing cold. Every now and then we recognise a stretch we've been on before. The wind and the current are making it impossible to figure out the layout of this ice maze.

Then, all of a sudden, we hear the voice of the communications officer over the radio. The connection is still appalling, but we can make out the words 'adaptor… Pelican case…' before he falls away again.

'Daniel, have another look in that case. Is there an adaptor under the foam by any chance?' I ask.

The bosun turns the case inside out and extracts an adaptor. Lo and behold, it fits the 12V charger in the middle console. Goodness, I can't believe we didn't think of this before. We blame it on the cold and the fatigue. This time we do get through on the sat phone. Captain Watson promises to wait for us if it's absolutely necessary, but he'd prefer to stay behind the *Nisshin Maru*. We're told to hurry up and given new coordinates. Daniel relays the instructions and Simon changes our course. The sky clears a little, so we can actually see a few hundred metres ahead. Once our driver has found a route to open water, the Gemini tears across the sea at 40 knots. At long last, our home base is in sight.

After more than 9 hours on the freezing cold water of Antarctica, we finally set foot on board the *Steve Irwin* again. Not everything went according to plan, but we did prevent the harpoon ship from hunting. The ship's cook greets us with mugs of hot soy chocolate. We gulp down the warm liquid like a herd of parched and knackered horses. And once we've hosed down and refuelled the Gemini, we're allowed to warm our freezing bodies under a blissfully hot shower. Three minutes, no longer.

19

THE BIG BANG

You might not know it sailing along this inhospitable continent, but Antarctica teems with life. At first sight it looks desolate: the bare rocks off the coast, the gigantic expanses of ice, the stiff wind that rarely subsides, the sub-zero temperatures and the icy cold sea – it all seems pretty hostile to living beings. Yet in this wilderness life shows its infinite capacity for survival.

It starts with the diatoms, the unicellular algae that cling to the underside of the ice. As soon as the floes melt in summer, the plankton pounce on the microscopically small nutrients. They in turn feed the krill that make up a large part of the diet of other sea fauna. Fish and cetaceans, especially, gorge on these small crustaceans. The fish fall prey to Weddell seals, leopard seals and various penguin species. The large baleen whales devour tons of krill, after which their faeces bring nutrients for the plankton to the water's surface. All along the edges of the ice, orcas hunt for seals and penguins. The chain is complete as soon as the whales die a natural death: the giants sink to the bottom of the ocean where they decompose into a feast for the scroungers down there. The krill gobble up the smallest creatures again and so the seemingly simple but actually fragile and complex life cycle around the South Pole starts all over again.

Simon, our on-board biologist, never tires of talking about the creatures of the Antarctic. But it's birds that really make his eyes light up. He spends hours on the afterdeck, making notes in his little notebook.

Of course I can see the difference between an albatross and a petrel, but in the end they're just birds to me. Not so for Simon. He will describe in detail the graceful flight of the sooty albatross taking advantage of our slipstream. Excited by everything he sees, he paces up and down the deck while swift grey petrels fly so low their wings skim the waves.

He points to snow petrels around the icebergs, which are chirping furiously in an attempt to drive us away. Once or twice the biologist thinks he has spotted a rare blue petrel and a broad-billed prion. Each bird has its own distinctive features, its own style. The more the scientist talks about his hobby, the more I enjoy listening to his voice.

One gorgeous summer afternoon, with the sun high and bright in the sky, Simon, Arne and I are standing on the bow, relishing the sight of two passing fin whales. As soon as one of their backs emerges from the water, we hear a loud whooshing sound. The whale's blowhole spews a plume of vapour up in the air.

'Wow, what a terrific sound,' I exclaim. 'This is so incredibly beautiful. Two of these giants swimming past and shattering the silence with their noise. You can feel it in your whole body. It takes you right back to the evolution of the planet, don't you think? The Big Bang encapsulated by the primeval sound of these mighty animals.'

'No, I can't say I do,' Simon says, looking baffled. Arne bursts out laughing. 'They're just breathing, stupid,' Simon continues.

'Seriously, the Big Bang, what are you on about?'

'You don't understand.'

'No, damn right I don't, ha ha… Big Bang… Loser!'

Arne wipes the tears from his eyes. I feel a little deflated as I watch the fun-poking duo walk away from me, laughing.

20

RESULT!

The Japanese factory ship is trying to shake off the Sea Shepherd vessel by luring us into fields of sea ice. The hull of the *Nisshin Maru* is much stronger and rounder than ours and has no trouble breaking through the pancake ice.

The crew thinks back to that hopeless situation a couple of weeks ago. Nobody wants to go through this dangerous ice mass. But we have no choice, because Captain Watson is determined to stay on the whaler's tail. As long as we're in their wake, we should be all right, the commanding officer reckons. But it's not long before our worst fears are realised and growlers start scraping past our bow again.

'I thought we'd learned our lesson,' Simon says, as he looks over the railing at the waterline. A large chunk of ice scrapes past the bow and is pushed aside. 'I'll do anything,' I moan, 'reckless stunts in a rubber boat, ramming, throwing, you name it, as long as we don't have to go through this bloody ice again.'

Unfortunately, it's not up to me to decide. The *Nisshin Maru* powers on and a couple of hours later we're smack in the middle of the sea ice. Our course is determined by the ship we hate. The whaler is steaming full force ahead.

Luckily for us, the whalers must have overestimated the size of the archipelago of ice, because after a couple of hours an enormous expanse of open water appears on the horizon. The factory ship has paved a way to the Ross Sea, a deep bay between Victoria Land and Marie Byrd Land. For the best part of the year this sea is frozen, but in summer much of the ice melts, causing the krill to proliferate. It's a paradise for the wildlife around Antarctica, most notably whales – something that has not gone unnoticed by Japan.

Now that we're out of the ice, three harpoon vessels follow us in formation. It doesn't matter, at least not for the moment, because as long as the hunters are in our vicinity no whales will perish. But it's too good to be true: the Japanese pass and disappear beyond the horizon.

At around 04.00 hours one of the quartermasters wakes the deckhands. The captain wants us to go after the *Nisshin Maru* to lure back and eliminate the harpoon vessels. Less than half an hour later we're in the water. Both the Gemini and the Delta race towards the processing ship. And even though it's the middle of the night, the sun is in the sky. The Ross Sea is a sheet of glass, there's not a breath of wind and no drift ice to be seen. At last, a perfect day for hunting the hunters.

Meanwhile our pilot is flying over the factory ship and he sounds worried. 'They're deploying the LRAD. They're pointing it at me. I can feel my whole body vibrating. I'm going to back off a bit. The thing's on port side.'

The Long Range Acoustic Device – we had a sneaking suspicion that the whalers had one on board, but hadn't seen it until now. The device emits high or low frequency audio waves. If the frequency is high the sound is mostly irritating; if low, it can cause nausea and even disorientation. The technology is used mainly by the police or military to disperse large crowds. It's best to stay away, but that's not an option if we want to get closer. We'll approach the *Nisshin* from starboard side.

As was the case a couple of days ago, we can't get the bottles of butyric acid over the railings of the *Nisshin Maru*. With all its protective netting, the huge ocean steamer has turned into an unassailable fortress. There's only one option left, but it will require a lot of nerve.

Simon drives the rubber boat several hundred metres ahead of the *Nisshin* before spinning it round. He stops a moment. The Gemini's engines growl, like an angry bull clawing the earth with its hooves. 'I'm gonna go fast, mate,' Simon yells. 'So hold on.'

Our tiny 7-metre boat is heading straight for the 135-metre *Nisshin Maru*. One piloting error and we'll slam against the factory ship at more than 60 kilometres per hour. I'm holding a bottle of butyric acid in my hands, ready to throw. This head-on approach gives us a couple of seconds outside the range of the water cannons. Just before we get to the bow, the Gemini veers sharply to the right and we narrowly cut across. The sizeable bow wave launches the rubber boat, sends it flying through the air and then lands it hard on the water. My bottle flies towards the deck. To no effect. The hull is far too high.

Still, our audacity has caught the attention of the harpoon vessels. They make straight for our rubber boat, like sharks to fresh blood. They're keen to protect the mother ship.

Our command immediately orders us to leave the *Nisshin* alone and to go after the *Yushin* vessels instead. Roger that. Our prey is harpoon ship *Yushin Maru No. 3*. We've got a new prop fouler on board; it's homemade, but hopefully it will do.

As soon as we approach, the harpoon ship makes off. Our driver takes advantage of the perfect weather conditions by zigzagging menacingly in front of the bow. The minute he briefly drops back

Freezing cold waves batter the Delta boat. (Photo © Adam Lau)

Laurens tries to contact mother ship *Steve Irwin* via the radio. (Photo © Eric Cheng)

A bollle of butyric acid flies towards the harpoon. It's a hit! (Photo © Adam Lau)

The Gemini narrowly misses the harpoon vessel as Laurens is about to throw. (Photo © Adam Lau)

The prop fouler is launched by bosun Daniel. (Photo © Adam Lau)

Opposite top The *Steve Irwin* is stuck in the ice. (Photo © Eric Cheng)

Opposite bottom Team Gemini, with the fleeing harpoon vessel *Nisshin Maru* in the background. (Photo © Adam Lau)

Above The Gemini ploughs through the Antarctic ice. (Photo © Steve Roest)

Opposite top The Gemini cuts across the harpoon vessel. The helicopter checks for dangerous ice floes. (Photo © Steve Roest)

Opposite middle Billboard announcing the second season of the popular TV series *Whale Wars*. (Photo © Animal Planet)

Opposite bottom The Sea Shepherd flag flies proudly at the Ross Ice Shelf. (Photo © Adam Lau)

Above A whale conservationist's nightmare: a minke whale is hauled up the factory ship's slipway. (Photo © Adam Lau)

Opposite top Laurens and the crew of *Whale Wars* on CNN's *Larry King Live*. (Photo © Sea Shepherd)

Opposite bottom Steve, Paul and Laurens stage a playful protest to challenge the 'scientific research'. (Photo © Deborah Bassett)

Above Visitors on the quay waiting to look on board the *Ady Gil*. (Photo © Laurens de Groot)

Above The *Ady Gil* finally reaches Antarctica. (Photo © Deborah Bassett)

Opposite The *Shonan Maru 2* ploughs through the *Ady Gil*. (Photo © Jo-Anne McArthur)

Top After the collision Laurens removes the flags. They mustn't fall into Japanese hands. (Photo © Sea Shepherd)

Bottom Flagship *Steve Irwin* in front of the Ross Ice Shelf, with the damage from the collision to the right. (Photo © Andy Lau)

Opposite top Some of the members of the desert team on the beach prior to their mission. (Photo © Laurens de Groot)

Opposite bottom Back to Namibia, now with an entirely new weapon: the drone. (Photo © Jake Weber)

At Cape Cross: a young Cape fur seal cries for its mother. (Photo © Laurens de Groot)

alongside the vessel, we hear a shrill, deafening beeping from the harpooner: the LRAD. As soon as Simon steers away from the side the sound fades. They gave us a bit of a shock, but the high frequency tones don't really bother anyone. The Gemini moves closer again, but maintains enough of a distance for the sound to be irritating but not dangerous. Richard shrugs it off: 'I've been to house parties where the noise was a lot worse.' Looking at his lean, lived-in face, I don't doubt that at all.

We've agreed with our command to use a different frequency each time we have radio contact so the Japanese don't jam us again. Officer Hammarstedt shouts over the radio: 'Tora, tora, tora!' Within seconds, our prop fouler flies out of the wheelie bin. The *Yushin Maru* thunders over it at 20 knots. Above us, Chris cheers: 'I can't see it. I reckon it's under.' We keep a nervous eye on the back of the harpoon vessel. Chris removes any doubt: 'It's in the propeller. I can see the rope trailing behind them. Well done, guys.'

At last. At last! At long last we've eliminated one of these wretched ships. The *Yushin Maru* grinds to a halt. The incapacitated vessel bobs up and down in the water, while we're tracing circles of joy. Clearly panicking, the whale killers rush to the stern. A pole with an underwater camera is lowered into the water.

But we don't get to sit back and relax. Hammarstedt comes over the radio: 'Well done, Gemini. Please return to base. The other *Yushins* are trying to cut off the *Steve*.'

'Copy that,' I reply. The great weather allows us to race back at 40 knots. The Gemini's 400 horses gallop bravely across the Ross Sea. Bring on the next hunter!

The *Yushin Maru 1* and *Yushin Maru 2* are circling the *Steve Irwin*. They're trying to cut her off so the *Nisshin Maru* can increase its distance. So far they have failed to do so, but their manoeuvres are extremely dangerous. The whale war has degenerated into a battle for Antarctica. The commander asks us to come back on board with the Gemini. It's a shame, but perfectly understandable, because if they have to wait for us later, we'll lose sight of the *Nisshin*. In order to recover us and to avoid the harpoon vessels, the *Steve Irwin* is forced to sail in circles. The crane operator will have to lift the Gemini on board while the ship is doing 15 knots to starboard. A pretty risky undertaking, and never attempted before.

Before I click the bowline into the carabiner of our painter, five crew members climb the rope ladder up to the deck. The stern line must be secured now. One of the harpoon vessels is coming closer and closer. Its bow wave lifts the Gemini and slams it hard against the *Steve Irwin*. Simon and I struggle to remain upright. 'Hurry up!' we hear from the bridge. As if we need to be told. We ignore it. The second hunter approaches and tries to screw us with a bow wave on the inside.

'Hold on,' I yell at Simon, who doesn't see the wave. He looks over his shoulder and fails to spot the hook, which is just being lowered by the crane. 'Watch out!' Simon ducks and the heavy hook narrowly misses his head.

I quickly snatch the hook and click it into a connector bringing four steel wires together. The crane jib swings up and pulls three of the wires taut. The fourth gets stuck behind a seat. Gravity yanks at the seat, pulling it out of the deck. The Gemini tilts and very nearly chucks us out of the boat. Just as the bolts are about to be ripped out, I tug at the steel cable. It snaps free and whips back hard against my hand. A cry, but no pain, because I'm so cold I can't feel a thing. The crane operator parks the Gemini against the bulwark and Simon and I jump on deck.

'That was insane,' Simon says, visibly upset. 'Really dodgy.'

'The bastards! Did you see how close those morons got? Give me a whaler and I'll sock him in the face.' I don't give a shit about the whirring cameras. My torrent of abuse continues until the ship's doctor arrives. My hand. I'd forgotten all about it.

'I can't feel a thing, Doc. It's the cold.'

'Nothing's bent out of shape. Does this hurt?' He squeezes the ball of my hand.

'Maybe, but I don't feel anything.'

'Can you move your fingers?'

'With difficulty.'

'I don't think it's broken, just badly bruised. Go and warm up. I'll strap up your hand afterwards.' I don't need to be told twice. Warming up on doctor's orders – I couldn't ask for a better prescription.

The rubber boat actions are over. The whalers are becoming more brazen and more aggressive by the day. If we were to launch the boats again, we'd only be tempting fate.

Sea Shepherd continues to chase the whaling fleet due south. We've now passed the 70th degree of latitude. The conservation society's ships have never been as far south as this. The landscape here is desolate and a long, long way from civilisation. This is the end of the world. And in this barren wilderness we're fighting a bunch of wild poachers who are growing more and more reckless every day. Escalation is inevitable. How it happens remains to be seen.

Pedro, quartermaster on the bridge, quotes an explorer whose name has slipped his mind. It captures our situation in a nutshell: 'Below 50 degrees south, there is no law. Below 60 degrees south, there is no hope. Below 70 degrees south, there is no God.'

We're sailing at a latitude of 74 degrees south. A harpoon vessel goes after a minke whale. Our maker doesn't notice.

21

THIS FAR AND NO FURTHER

Position: 75° 42' S, 165° 27' W.

At dawn there's a loud knock on our cabin door: 'They're catching whales, they're catching whales,' Amber screams hysterically.

'Huh, what?' Pottsy and I wake up dazed from our brief sleep, so well deserved after our tiring actions against the whaling fleet. As soon as the message has sunk in, we quickly slip into Mustang suits and run onto the deck to see what's going on.

Photographer Steve Roest is leaning over the bulwark, peering at the whale processor. His face is ashen. 'I never expected this,' he says, full of disgust. 'For them to be catching whales right in front of our noses. I can't think of a greater provocation. They're hacking a minke whale to pieces right now.' Fountains of blood gush from the sides of the *Nisshin Maru*.

'Which ship delivered the whale?' I ask. The question is pointless, I know, and it probably sounds gauche, but I feel I have to say something.

'The *Yushin Maru 3*.'

'What the fuck, how's that possible? We fouled her prop yesterday!'

'They seem to have disentangled the rope. They're really here. In fact, all three harpoon vessels are busy hunting.'

'You're joking...' My spirits plummet. The whalers no longer fear the big black pirate ship that chases them every hunting season. Whereas in previous years they took to their heels, this year they're doing the exact opposite. It's a first. So much for our prop foulers and butyric acid: fed up, the whalers now simply ignore us. Today marks the start of the hunting season and all we can do for now is stand back and watch.

'What do you think Watson will do?'

'No idea, but you don't want to be anywhere near him. In all his 30 years of campaigning, he's never seen anyone harpoon a whale. I've no idea what effect this bloodbath will have on him.'

I feel for our captain. He's dedicated his life to protecting the friendly giants of the sea. Sometimes successfully, sometimes less so. Until now, this campaign had gone to plan. The whale processor had been fleeing us for weeks and the harpoon vessels were powerless.

The Sea Shepherd crew watch as dozens of Japanese cut the whale into pieces. The meat is stripped off the thick layer of blubber and immediately taken to the freezers. In a couple of months' time it will reappear at the Tokyo fish market. Ribs and guts are tossed overboard. Petrels are dancing up in the sky and picking at the free meal floating on the water. As we follow in the *Nisshin Maru*'s wake, we see entrails drifting past the *Steve Irwin*.

Yesterday's jubilant mood has turned funereal. On deck, the ship's cook is staring at the whaler with tears in her eyes. 'Incredible,' she says. 'Even we can't stop them? I thought one of the privileges of sailing with Sea Shepherd was that you wouldn't see any whales being slaughtered. I guess that was an illusion.'

There are no happy faces in the pilothouse either. One of the cameramen is taking close-ups of the intense emotions. The officers are dumbstruck as they watch the floating slaughterhouse, upset and struggling with unexpected feelings of pure hatred.

Helicopter pilot Chris takes off to film the processing from up close. He describes what we'd already witnessed. The skill with which the whalers cut one of the world's largest mammals to pieces within minutes has been raised to a cruel art form. These Japanese workers do little else all year. Once the fishing season in the Southern Ocean has come to an end they sail back to empty the Japanese waters.

The pilot's attention is caught by a distant harpoon vessel doing a sudden turn. Inadvertently he witnesses the most horrific spectacle an anti-whaler could ever see.

'Bridge, this is the helicopter, over.'

'Go ahead, helicopter.'

'I'm at your three o'clock and I'm following the *Yushin Maru No. 3*. I think it's starting again.'

'Roger.'

The crew is silent. Worried. We all dread Chris's next words.

'Oh my God. Two minke whales are swimming in front of the bow. They're fleeing the ship at 17 knots. One of the whalers is at the harpoon. The animals are so frantic they can't get a big enough breath to dive. They're swimming for their lives.'

The harpoon vessel zigzags through the water without losing sight of the whales. Despite its beautifully streamlined body, the *Balaenoptera bonaerensis* is no match for the modern engines of the Japanese whaler. The *Yushin* is going after one of the minke whales, forcing the animal to keep coming up on starboard side. The other one gets away. At least for now. More and more plumes of vapour shoot up out of the water. The whale is losing its breath, and it's losing the battle. Its back emerges for one last breath of air.

'He's got his hand on the trigger. Oh my God, this is something I thought I'd never see… oh my God.' A deafening explosion echoes across the Antarctic water, as the harpoon pierces the minke whale's small body and rips apart its flesh and entrails. The whale slips under the water and thrashes about to escape the meat hook in its body.

'He just shot it.'

Dead silence on the bridge. Captain Watson is staring straight ahead, absolutely heartbroken. We'd been promised that if we found the factory ship, no whales would get shot. But now our worst nightmare is coming true: the whalers are laughing right in the face of Sea Shepherd. Our captain, the leading conservationist feared by poachers and known to sink ships, is being made to look like a fool. The hunters are winning.

The small minke whale surfaces. It's floating in a pool of its own blood, which is gushing from its wound. The seawater turns red in a big circle around the dying animal. It gasps for breath, but in vain. The harpoon has inflicted a fatal wound just behind its head. Its strength is ebbing away. The struggling animal is fighting an unequal battle. And all the while the Japanese leisurely draw in their harpoon line.

The harpoon gunner walks to the bow with a rifle in his hands. He looks quite full of himself. A shot follows. Another one. And another one. He fires no less than six times until the animal finally dies, 30 minutes after the harpoon was fired.

The *Yushin Maru* 3 stops its engines. The minke whale dangles lifeless from a cable at the bow. Deckhands fasten the whale to the side of the ship. Its fluke protrudes from the water, looking like a trophy displayed by the triumphant Japanese crew. The rest of its body dangles under water. The dead minke whale will have to be transferred to the *Nisshin Maru* within the next couple of hours, or else the cadaver will start decomposing.

'Bridge, the whale is dead. I'm returning to base.' That's all Chris says.

On the bridge, Captain Watson is no longer staring glumly into space; the fire is back in his eyes. The sheer determination with which he led us through the ice, with which he's been sailing the seas for 30 years, can be heard in his firm words: 'That whale is not going on board the *Nisshin Maru.*'

22

ON COLLISION COURSE!

The *Steve Irwin* is tearing across the calm Ross Sea, her prow pointed at the *Nisshin Maru*. The Sea Shepherd ship is approaching from the right, the *Yushin Maru No. 3* is coming from the left. The harpoon vessel is only a few hundred metres from the *Nisshin*'s slipway. Arriving late is not an option. The shot minke whale mustn't be unloaded. The harpoon vessel slows down, while the crew on deck walks to and fro with all kinds of ropes. They're ready to transfer the whale. We're just a few dozen metres from the hunter.

'It's going to be tight,' Watson says gravely. 'I'm not moving. It's a game of chicken now.'

The *Steve Irwin* and the *Yushin Maru No. 3* are on a collision course. Unless one of us gives way, we're headed for a terrible crash.

'Hang on,' the message spreads through the ship. I'm on deck, clutching one of the pillars under the helicopter deck and bracing myself for a shock. None is forthcoming. The captain of the Japanese vessel chooses the lesser of two evils and veers to port.

'Hah! We did it,' the other deckies and I whoop for joy.

The *Steve Irwin* settles in the wake of the *Nisshin Maru*, determined not to budge. On the afterdeck Arne rubs his hands gleefully in the knowledge that the captain has pulled it off. 'It was about time they got scared again. When all else fails, we can only use our own ship to protect the whales. And we'll do so if we have to.'

There are no dissenting voices among the activists; we all agree with the captain's radical course. This is our final chance. We've done everything in our power to tell the illegal whalers to clear out of the South Pole sanctuary. It looks as if we have to jeopardise our own ship to get the message across.

The *Yushin Maru* pulls away from us. When it's several hundred metres away, it makes an unexpected U-turn and positions itself behind the *Steve Irwin* for a while. The dead minke whale is still being towed through the water on port side. The frantic activity on the Japanese deck suggests that the crew refuse to give up. According to the deckhands on our afterdeck they're going to make another attempt.

Bosun Daniel wants some of us on the bow with butyric acid. The photographer rushes forward. Pottsy wants to go out on the bow, and goes inside to drum up other volunteers. Because of my bandaged hand I can't hold the bottles properly, so if it comes to action, I'm going to have to stand by and watch. Very frustrating.

Meanwhile, one of the quartermasters has made his way down from the bridge for a briefing. 'As soon as they try to transfer the whale, we'll position ourselves between the *Yushin Maru* and the *Nisshin Maru*. We'll try to sever the ropes used in the transfer. This could get nasty.' He concludes with nervous laughter.

'It's coming,' Simon yells from the afterdeck as the *Yushin Maru* approaches. I go in search of a good spot on the afterdeck, where I can see everything but also brace myself. Pottsy runs past with a bottle of butyric acid. He rushes to the bow and takes up his position.

The harpooner passes us on port side – quite easily, as these vessels are superior to the *Steve Irwin*. As it cuts across, the ship misses our bow by a hair's breadth. You can say what you want, but the Japanese captain has some guts too. Or else he's still in a blind rage because we fouled his prop a couple of days ago. Either way, he seems determined to transfer the whale.

The *Yushin* positions itself to the right behind the processing ship. The crew quickly ties a line between the whaler and the factory ship. Hurriedly, while the *Steve Irwin* is closing in, they secure the whale carcass. They're working so incredibly fast, our time to intercept the transfer is running out.

We all feel that the *Steve Irwin* is moving at a snail's pace as it sails alongside. And every Japanese crew member who's not dealing with the whale is hurling stuff at the Sea Shepherd crew. Tools, nuts, bits of lead and golf balls: the men and women on our bow are dodging all kinds of objects. We pay them back with butyric acid.

The sight of the dead whale stirs a lot of anger in me. I mutter out loud what every crew member is thinking: 'Ram it in the arse, captain. Come on. Give that ship a kick up the arse.' Nobody gives a monkey's about the consequences. This is what it's all about. If we flinch now all our work will have been for nothing.

That must be the thinking on the bridge too, because the *Steve Irwin* keeps going and smashes at full speed into the whaler's side. Creaking loudly, our prow slides over the whaler's railing. The Japanese crew scatter and take cover. The pressure on the *Yushin Maru* causes the *Steve Irwin* to list heavily to port. I cling to the railing as gravity tugs at my legs. Further along, I see Pottsy holding on with one hand and throwing a bottle of butyric acid with the other. The photographer is ensconced behind the gunwale, holding up his camera and clicking away without actually looking. The engines, which are roaring at full power, thrust the *Steve* further up the whaler's deck. It feels as if we're about to capsize.

The seconds seem to crawl by, but in reality everything happens at lightning speed. The *Steve Irwin* slides off the *Yushin Maru* before manoeuvring around the back and to the right. When we fall back, we see that we were a split second too late. The minke whale slides up the slipway and onto the *Nisshin Maru*'s flensing deck. Blood drips down into the sea. Having unloaded its catch, the harpoon ship leaves the battle scene and disappears beyond the horizon.

Our ship has sustained only limited damage. The anchor, one of her strongest components, took the worst of it. There's a hole just above the waterline, and with each swell quite a lot of water gushes through, but it's not a serious problem. Our skilled engineers weld it shut. Undaunted, we go after the whaler.

Although we failed to stop the transfer this time, our last-ditch attempt appears to have had an effect. The whalers had such a fright that no harpoon ship ventures anywhere near us now. All three sail at more than 14 miles from the *Nisshin Maru*.

We trail the revolting factory ship until we're almost down to our last drop of diesel. No blood pours from its scuppers. At long last, the whales of Antarctica are safe.

23

FAREWELL, ANTARCTICA

The Ross Ice Shelf rises high above the water. Before us, as far as the eye can see, hundreds of kilometres of ice stretch out in either direction. Deep crevices run from the sea straight to the top of the plateau. Every now and then, small pieces calve off this gigantic wall of ice and drop into the sea with a loud splash. This wonder of the natural world is the last we'll see of this gorgeous sanctuary and its inhabitants before we're forced to turn back.

A final flurry of the strong, katabatic wind blows the snow onto a small heap on the edge of the ice shelf. The sun shines low over the ice fields and casts a long shadow across the Ross Sea. The brilliant, whirling snow crystals top the enormous ice shelf with a sparkling diamond crown.

I've never seen anything quite like it. Here, at the far end of the world, nature has built a dome of pristine white ice. We only get to see a fraction of the frozen mass, but it's enough to make me feel very small and very insignificant. In the midst of eternity, my soul is permeated with a sense of mortality – we represent a mere nanosecond in the history of this remarkable planet. And yet, as human beings, we're capable of destroying the earth in a blink. A sobering thought.

But there's no place for such thoughts. Not here. Not now. In the shadow of this ice shelf I'm surrounded by people who are trying to make a difference in this blink of life. The presence of positive conservationists is an inexhaustible source of inspiration to me and pushes any pessimism to the background.

While the *Steve Irwin* slowly points its prow northwards, I'm reminded of a quote from Mother Teresa: 'We ourselves feel that what we are doing is just a drop in the ocean. But the ocean would be less because of that missing drop.'

Our position is 77° 53' S and 178° 03' W. I'm unlikely to ever make it further south in my lifetime. We're less than 13 degrees from the Geographic South Pole. Behind this wall of ice lurks a brutal landscape where no man can survive without protection. For a moment I forget our whale wars. I have now crossed the Southern Ocean, the most ferocious ocean in the world, five times and have conquered fears and taken risks that have exceeded my wildest expectations. From now on adventure will always be in my blood.

A total of 305 whales were saved during Operation Miyamoto Musashi, the Japanese Institute for Whale Research announced after the whaling fleet returned. That's to say, the institute admitted a shortfall of 305 whales and blamed it on Sea Shepherd. There's no greater compliment than that.

24

ROCK 'N' ROLL USA

'*Whale Wars* splashes across the increasingly exhausted genre of people-at-work reality series like icy seawater, jolting you awake with a frothy, briny burst of – well, you get the idea. This is one spunky show.'

Neil Genzlinger in *The New York Times*

'What? Pull up!' Our driver does as he's told and parks the limousine on the hard shoulder of the West Side Highway in New York. Looking back through the open roof I can see an enormous billboard beside the motorway.

'How cool is that? We're on a billboard, guys!' The advertisement announces the new season of *Whale Wars*: crew member Shannon Mann is standing next to me in a rubber boat, while a whaler closes in on us in the background.

It's not a campaign photo. On the contrary. A couple of weeks ago, Shannon and I found ourselves modelling in a studio in San Francisco: make-up, false beard, a bicycle wheel for a helm, a wobbly plank to simulate movement and a camp assistant pointing a fan at my hair while at the same time squirting it with a plant spray. A very close approximation of our Antarctic hardships indeed.

The end result can be seen in all its glory beside the motorway en route to JFK Airport. It shows me in a savage yelling pose. The poster seems to advertise a film about wild marauders instead of a series featuring peace-loving activists. But never mind, Animal Planet was satisfied.

After a promotional appearance in New York City, the next item on our agenda is a meeting with Arianna Huffington of the Huffington Post. The limousine drops us off at the airport. Captain Watson and crew members Shannon Mann, Chris Aultman and I have been travelling around the States for months to promote Sea Shepherd and the TV series. Imagine entering the United States as an activist and then going on to lead a high-octane jet-set lifestyle. Not that I'm complaining.

How did all this come about? In Hobart, immediately after the end of Operation Musashi, Shannon invited me to dinner with fellow crew member Steve Roest and the New Zealander Rob Holden. Both Sea Shepherd supporters wanted to help the organisation raise funds.

They invited me because I like a challenge, get on well with Watson and am friends with Shannon. Before we've even had our starter, Rob cuts to the chase: 'Do you like a gamble?'

'Yes,' I reply keenly. I can't wait to hear what's next. 'Good, how would you like to spend some time in the States to work on two things? One, help Paul Watson get in shape. He's too heavy and needs to lose some weight. You do martial arts training, right?'

'Uh huh.'

'Well then, I'm sure you can train with him while also assisting us with our fundraising efforts. I'm planning to organise events and generate money for a new ship. Within the next three years, Sea Shepherd has to raise at least $100 million. You won't get paid, but you'll be given accommodation and expenses. What do you think?'

A terrific offer. An adventure in the States is really tempting, although it also presents me with a dilemma: if I'm selfish and go for adventure, it will spell the end of my relationship, that's for sure.

A handshake seals it: we're going to raise the money for a new ship.

The metropolis that is Melbourne is swapped for tiny Friday Harbor on the San Juan Islands in Washington State. Walk around the streets of this sparsely populated village and you'll see fat four-wheel drives and often even fatter residents. This is a small and close-knit community, which is confirmed after our first visit to Herbs, the local pub.

Karaoke on Wednesdays, a baseball game or bowling on Saturdays and church on Sundays are the weekly highlights in the village. In summer the island fills with nature lovers keen to see the world-famous wild orcas, while in winter Friday Harbor is deserted, its population halved. Young people either take to drugs or seek their fortune on the mainland, while senior citizens spend their grey dollars on a retirement place.

So initially my new job is hardly bursting with excitement. The Sea Shepherd headquarters are tucked away in the woods, just outside Friday Harbor. Based in a converted bed and breakfast, the organisation employs around 15 people who keep the it afloat. Captain Watson lives in a room next to the offices. The employees are friendly and always pleased to see crew members pop by to talk about their experiences in the field. Shannon and I like to go there, but at the end of the day we're always just that little bit happier to return to the spacious villa our sponsor has rented for us in the hills outside the village. Its splendid view of the valley and magnificent veranda make us feel like royalty in Friday Harbor. With a palace like this, you naturally prefer to work from home.

Having spent a couple of days acclimatising, I start Watson on his fitness routine: long walks, squash, fitness and a healthy diet. The walks and games of squash agree with the Sea Shepherd founder, but the machines in the gym are wasted on him. Besides, after every week of training our figurehead is off somewhere to give talks or wheedle donations out of people. This way, the sessions have little or no effect. Save for the occasional walk or game of squash, the fitness ideals are gradually abandoned. It soon transpires that I'd better focus on my second brief: fundraising.

A sponsor in the Hollywood Hills has put his house (read: huge mansion) at our disposal for a benefit event. Our mission: to raise money for a new ship. Sea Shepherd has its eye on the *Earthrace*. This futuristic-looking vessel, a unique wave-piercing trimaran, can pull more than 40 knots. Its current owner, Pete Bethune, is prepared to sell the ship to the conservation society so the activists can zip down to Antarctica in no time at all. Our team is supposed to raise the asking price of $1,000,000.

During the preparations for the event, the *Earthrace* skipper visits Friday Harbor to meet Watson. My first impression of the New Zealander as he gets off the ferry is that of a jolly sea dog. Lively, twinkling eyes in a lean face suggest a hunger for a new adventure. A bald head, impressive Maori tattoos on his arms, a T-shirt with cropped sleeves and sea-weathered cargo trousers complete the picture of a dyed-in-the-wool mariner. Even his language is that of a rough seaman: raw and without the usual niceties.

Pete talks non-stop about everything he's got in store for the whalers. And he doesn't mince his words. Most of his plans are rubbish, but his enthusiasm is infectious. I reckon that with all of his experience, the New Zealander is an excellent addition to our South Pole team. Two days later, Pete leaves the island to start preparing for the lengthy expedition.

All we need now is the money. To create a strong pre-sell effect, our team photoshops a great poster of the *Earthrace* decked out Sea Shepherd-style. It does the trick on the night of the benefit. The celebrities in the Hollywood arbour swoon at the sight of the cool, futuristic boat. Sea Shepherd manages to raise $100,000. The seed for the idea of the *Earthrace* as our harpoon interceptor is germinating.

Several of the crew members who feature in *Whale Wars* have come over for the event. The 'reality soapies' have caught the attention of Animal Planet, which wants to use this opportunity to promote the TV series. Sea Shepherd jumps at the chance and we do talk show after talk show.

The highlight of our publicity campaign is an appearance on *Larry King Live*. CNN's legendary talk show host has invited Captain Watson, Chris, Shannon and myself to talk about our most recent campaign. The four of us are seated at a table in the CNN studio in Los Angeles. Our host is sitting opposite us, fiddling with his microphone. The taping starts in a couple of minutes' time. With his large head, which is disproportionate to his small body, Larry reminds me of Gollum from *The Lord of the Rings*.

Just before we're due to begin, he leans forward a bit and stares at me with those piercing eyes of his. Then he points his notorious finger at me: 'Your name is Laurens, right?' He says it the English way, Lawrence. Slightly taken aback, I answer in the affirmative. 'Well, my name is Lawrence too,' he says. He laughs at that and leans back again, relaxed. 'We've got something in common.' The ice has been broken.

The director shouts '20 seconds', which is a cue for everybody to start fidgeting in their chairs, clearing throats and releasing final nervous coughs. Although the show isn't live, it's watched by millions. Of course we're nervous.

But I'm not nearly as nervous as I was a couple of weeks before on the Dutch TV show *Pauw & Witteman*. A million viewers and my family scrutinising my every word: boy, was I tense. With gushing armpits, a face virtually pulled apart by nervous tics and a jacket borrowed off a Discovery Channel staffer who thought I couldn't appear dressed in a grungy T-shirt, I reported on Operation Musashi.

But now we're with Larry. One by one, he works his way through the questions. I trot out the same old answers, more or less on automatic pilot after all the interviews with weeklies, dailies and radio and TV journalists: former police detective, the whalers are poachers, we're catching crooks, we use non-violent methods and we refuse to be cowed.

The interview is in the can. Upon exiting the studio, we're each given one of the much-coveted black microphone mugs that are always on the table during Larry King's interviews. The mug is for my father, who can finally muster some respect for my work after watching the broadcast.

A couple of weeks after the fundraiser in LA we strike gold. The philanthropic entrepreneur Ady Gil is donating the astronomic sum of $1,000,000, so we can buy the *Earthrace*. The ship is renamed the *Ady Gil* and immediately readied for a trip to the South Pole. It's going to be a very hazardous expedition. The ship's hull is made of carbon fibre and every ice floe could prove fatal for the fragile trimaran. In fact, crossing the Southern Ocean in a 24-metre boat is a huge challenge in itself – and that's putting it mildly.

Getting the material ready is one thing, but finding a crew for the *Ady Gil* will be a tall order. When news of our purchase spreads around the Sea Shepherd ranks, nobody comes forward of their own accord. Few have faith in a successful expedition to Antarctica. Informally, the *Earthrace* is rechristened the 'Deathrace'.

After our media blitz I stay in Los Angeles for a while, basking in the glow of the semi-celebrity lifestyle. Just about every evening there's some event where Sea Shepherd representatives are allowed to put in an appearance. This finds me having a beer with the world-famous singer Jason Mraz at the Liquid Nation Ball, or backstage at a gig, chatting to hip-hop legend Ice-T about our adventures. The Sea Shepherd crew shirt serves as an access-all-areas pass. People who achieve something in real life are a welcome addition to the world of film, glamour and plastic. The invitations for promotional talks keep pouring in.

Needless to say, founder Watson remains the biggest icon of the conservationists. With his imposing physique and characteristic skipper's head he catches people's attention wherever he goes, and instantly hugs the limelight. In the captain's presence his assistants can expect no more than a limp handshake from the celebs and wealthy of this earth, who are all queuing to have their picture taken with the environmental hero.

That Watson is the big shot is underlined at Sea No Evil, a huge art festival in aid of Sea Shepherd held in Riverside, Los Angeles. As soon as he strolls in a swarm of supporters makes straight for the queen bee. The *Whale Wars* fans hover around him until everybody is in possession of either a photo or an autograph. Any airs and graces shown by the other *Whale Wars* characters – the real-life activists – are brutally crushed in the presence of Captain Watson.

But whereas the captain is given the red-carpet treatment in the USA, he's less popular elsewhere in the world. Every year, the activist is declared *persona non grata* at the annual meeting of the International Whaling Commission (IWC). Sea Shepherd has been a thorn in the side of Japan and Norway for years now and the two countries have done everything in their power to ban the conservation society. And so they have in Madeira this year. Still, Watson is a constant presence around the meetings – in the lobby or, if necessary, outside, at the entrance to this farce which is financed with taxpayers' money and which has no sanctioning powers to deal with the countries that violate the regulations.

In Funchal, Japan once again dominates proceedings and claims to be carrying out painstaking scientific research. Peter Garrett,

Australia's Environment Minister, had earlier pledged to vehemently oppose this, but he fails to live up to his promise.

Steve Roest, who has climbed the ranks to become Sea Shepherd CEO, and myself decide to expose this travesty in a fun, light-hearted way. We buy two inflatable rubber boats, cut out the bottoms and daub 'Research Vessel' on the sides. We also fashion harpoons out of foam. Then, armed with the harpoons and wearing the boats like a bumper, we enter the Pestana Casino Park Hotel.

The black suits with dark sunglasses and earpieces at the entrance have heart attacks on the spot. The activists keep going. Never waver in the heat of the battle. The meeting is on the first floor. Steve makes for the lift, I take the stairs. While he's waiting for the lift doors to open, the Englishman finds himself surrounded by an army of bruisers. For a while he manages to dodge the security staff, but eventually he is escorted to the exit, with boat and all. I sneak upstairs.

The meeting has just been adjourned for lunch and the unsuspecting delegates are leaving the room. Peter Garrett, there he is… I run after him and ask if I can take DNA samples to check if the delegates are fit to protect whales. The photographers snap a picture for the papers. Garrett escapes with a faint smile. On to the Japanese. They too fall prey to my relentless harpoon. Panicking, they scatter in all directions. I immediately have security on my back. While flashing a disarming smile I tell them we're only doing research. The gorillas are not amused and hand me over to the police. On the pavement outside the hotel, Steve is busy conferring with a police commissioner, explaining our research purposes to him. The officers frogmarch us off the premises. We're not arrested, but they do slap a ban on us. The usually rather stern-looking police officers laugh when we slink off in our rubber outfits. They could see the funny side of our tongue-in-cheek action. So could the press. The IWC delegates a lot less so.

Back in Los Angeles, Rob informs us of our next mission. Friends in Las Vegas would like to organise a benefit for Sea Shepherd.

Shannon and I accept the challenge and the following day we drive to Nevada with a selection of party supplies.

The host and hostess recently moved here from New Zealand. The couple live in a beautiful property with marble floors, statues and a pool in the back garden. Both care deeply about Sea Shepherd, but between the lines I read that it's also an excellent opportunity for them to make a name for themselves in this wealthy neighbourhood.

Unfortunately, family circumstances force Shannon to return to Canada a couple of days later. The organisation of the party for 150 guests now rests entirely on my shoulders. The couple only know a handful of neighbours, so it's up to me to fill the house.

To start with, I consult the Sea Shepherd database: five local supporters. A quick round of phone calls reveals that three companies are no longer in business, one supporter has moved and the final one isn't interested. Here I am, empty-handed, with only six weeks to organise a benefit for an ocean conservation society in a desert city, hundreds of kilometres from the sea, with the host not knowing a single soul and my partner in Canada.

In these circumstances you've got two options: throw in the towel and beat a quiet retreat – I considered it more than once – or not give in and pick up the phone, approach people in person and do the best you can. And pray for a small miracle.

Where to start? With celebrities. They're the big draw at events like these. At the top of my list is someone I secretly admire: Randy Couture, multiple Ultimate Fighting Champion and an American mixed martial arts legend. Since I can't get through on the phone, I drive to the Xtreme Couture Gym to join a training session and establish contact that way. Upon arrival I realise that it's been a while since my last workout. The musclemen stare at me. I bet they wonder what someone with incipient love handles is doing in their gym. I'm beginning to have second thoughts. Oh, fuck it, all or nothing. I slap $20 on the counter, enough to give me a full day of martial arts training.

It goes without saying that I'm wearing a Sea Shepherd shirt. Who knows, maybe it will catch somebody's eye. But soon enough I realise that nobody is here to chat. After the warm-up I'm completely whacked and in urgent need of artificial respiration. Only an hour and a half to go. Ninety minutes later I haul myself off the mat and onto a bench where I catch my breath, absolutely shattered.

After a self-administered resuscitation and a change of clothes I talk to the instructors. They're a bit more forthcoming now that this novice has shown some feeling for the sport, despite his rusty, even lousy performance. They promise to hand the invitation to Couture. And tomorrow they'll also put out a large box with gifts for the benefit auction. Mission accomplished.

The other guests are easier to get hold of. Hundreds of invitations are dispatched and I also receive help from a great team of volunteers from Los Angeles. Everything comes together just in time and on the big day more than a hundred guests walk the red carpet. 'Extravagant' is what the hostess asked for, and that's what she's got: gorgeous waitresses in feathered burlesque costumes, an Elvis Presley impersonator at the entrance, piano players in the back garden, whale ice sculptures dispensing shots and copious amounts of other alcohol. Vegas through and through.

Rob flies over from Los Angeles with some business people, intending to use the festive evening to shove a contract with a clothing manufacturer under Watson's nose. The television series has made the Sea Shepherd logo a hot item and every week there's yet another shady character eager for a piece of the pie. The Sea Shepherd CEO, who's also in attendance, picks the iron-clad contract to pieces. It results in visible tension between Steve and Rob and spells the imminent demise of our fundraising team. I don't care. The benefit is a success, the New Zealand couple are satisfied and I go and blow off steam on the Vegas Strip with the other volunteers.

After the party in Las Vegas I spend some time with a friend in Los Angeles. Now that all the benefit events are over and the promotional activities have come to an end, I'm beginning to feel a bit lost in the States. I don't fancy the prospect of spending all my time raising funds. But the question is: what next?

The answer comes from CEO Steve Roest. He calls me on Skype: 'Do you remember we bought the *Ady Gil*?'

'Sure, you mean the Deathrace.'

'That's the one. Pete has selected his crew, but we'd like some Sea Shepherd people on board as well. Jeff Hansen is going. Paul and I can think of only two other suitable candidates, Chuck and yourself. But Chuck is going to be the captain of our other new ship, the *Bob Barker*.' He pauses a second.

'Would you like to join the *Ady Gil*?'

The question is as unexpected as it is flattering.

'Your job is simple: keep an eye on Pete Bethune, find the *Nisshin Maru* and come back alive.'

Take the *Ady Gil* to Antarctica? Never before has a trimaran sailed to Antarctica. This is no ordinary campaign, this is a highly dangerous expedition.

'Oh, stop it… you know I'm going to say yes.'

'Ha ha, I know. It'll be a thrilling ride. I wish I could come along.'

'Yeah, sure.'

The Englishman grins broadly on screen. We both know that this is going to be a hellish journey, but the thirst for adventure banishes all thoughts of danger.

A couple of weeks later I swap my life of partying, fundraising, oversized villas and celebrities for a place on board the *Ady Gil*.

During a stopover in the Netherlands I'm taken down a peg or two by the Dutch and their common sense. I join my brother and best friend for a farewell beer in Café Pol in Rotterdam. Needless to say, I'm dressed in my Sea Shepherd finery, making eyes at beautiful women. Sea Shepherd jacket, Sea Shepherd T-shirt – only the pirate underpants are missing. On my way to the toilets, I spot a blonde who's lighting up the joint with her sparkling eyes. She's drop-dead gorgeous. I have to talk to her, so armed with American self-confidence I decide to go on the pull. On my way back out I walk in a wide arc to see if I can make eye contact. My attempt fails miserably, unless you count the rotund dragon at the entrance who smiles back at me.

Luckily, a little later the blonde and her friend come out to stand under the patio heaters. We start chatting and I try everything to impress her: former police detective, saver of whales, Sea Shepherd. No reaction. I point to the logo on my jacket. Still no sign of recognition. 'You mean you don't know the TV series *Whale Wars*?' 'No,' she responds drily. My last trump: name dropping. Larry King, Michelle Rodriguez, MacGyver, Jason Mraz, Ricky Martin and a bunch of other celebs I've met in the past year. She couldn't care less. My bragging is dismissed with the words 'aren't you a big shot?' spoken in a broad Rotterdam accent. Her beautiful eyes regard me coolly. She's happy to talk to me, but there's no spark. The Rotterdam beauty gives me her name, Andrea, and age, but no phone number or email address.

She leaves the pub and leaves me speechless in the cold. The rejection, the painful lesson in humility, hasn't gone unnoticed by my brother. And as befits a family member, he keeps rubbing it in until the early hours of the morning. The time has come for me to cool down at sea.

THE
EXPEDITION

*" We hope that one day the humpbacks –
the composers of the sea – will sing a song
about that peculiar black ship and its crew,
if only not to be forgotten. "*
LAURENS DE GROOT

25

THE DOOMED FOREST

Emma leads the way, clambering nimbly over the tree trunks on the winding path to Camp Flozza. The Australian activist has been living in the anti-logging protest camp in the Tasmanian Upper Florentine Valley for months. She just picked us up by the side of the asphalt road linking the Styx Valley with the Gordon River Road. We've been invited by the Green Party in Hobart to attend the annual Walk Against Warming, a global warming protest march.

The tree activists are delighted that we're dropping by to show our support. Now that whaling is receiving so much attention in Australia, they're hoping we can help them spread their message.

Since we've been confined to just a couple of square metres on the *Ady Gil*, we're relieved to be away from our tiny boat. But at the same time we wish we weren't here at all. Our new boat should have been in Antarctica by now, but setbacks have forced us to return to Hobart twice without anything to show for our efforts.

The first time we'd only been away a couple of hours when we received orders to turn back. The reason wasn't immediately clear to us. But then it turned out that our other new ship, the *Bob Barker*, had been held up leaving Africa. We had to wait, because we were meant to reach the South Pole at the same time.

Our second attempt was thwarted by equipment failure. We'd been escorted out of the harbour by a pod of lively dolphins, but after about 24 hours the boat hit heavy weather with swells of several metres. Not a problem for the *Steve Irwin*, but all the more so for the small, 24-metre wave-piercer. Coping in this whirling washing machine became a baptism of fire for the seven-man crew.

For Antarctica veteran Jeff Hansen it was a hellish experience. After only a couple of hours at sea, the Australian withdrew into our tiny toilet at the back of the ship, only coming out when our cameraman had to throw up.

When an unexpectedly high wave smashed our radar to smithereens, we were forced to turn back. Upon our return to port, Jeff immediately left the ship. He had to admit that he wouldn't be able to handle this for months on end. These had been his toughest hours at sea ever.

The cameraman had to disembark as well. After two aborted attempts it suddenly dawned on Animal Planet just how dangerous this trip to Antarctica was going to be. Their lawyers weren't too keen on claims for damages should anything go wrong. The cameraman and his cameras wouldn't come back on board until we'd reached Antarctica. In the meantime we'd have to take our own photos.

The next test was put off until the arrival of a new radar. In an effort to boost morale, Captain Pete Bethune decided to visit our fellow activists in the Tasmanian rain forest.

'You're smelling *Eucalyptus regnans*. They're planning to cut down 50 hectares of those. They've named this stretch of ancient primeval forest FO044A,' our guide tells us as we turn into a sandy path which is partially covered in gravel. Caterpillar tracks indicate that this road has been constructed by the loggers for taking heavy machinery into the forest.

A car without wheels is parked in the middle of the road. The doors of the wreck are covered in graffiti with slogans saying 'NO MORE LOGGING' and 'SAVE THE OLD GROWTH'. Inside, a girl has chained her arm to the frame. She's planning to stay put until the authorities remove her. We wish her all the best with her brave attempt at thwarting the loggers. She wishes us luck in Antarctica.

Further up, the road is blocked by a spider's web of steel cables leading to a pole in the middle of the road. 'These cables are connected to platforms in the trees,' Emma explains. 'If one of them is cut it causes a platform to collapse and someone to fall out of the tree. The activists are putting their lives on the line to protect this forest.' The small wooden platforms have been nailed to the branches of the eucalyptus trees. Some of the rickety constructions are more than 50 metres up.

'The activists live and sleep in these small tree huts for weeks on end.'

'How do they pee?' is the first question that pops into my mind.

'Peeing and shitting is done in a bucket. When it's full the tree sitters winch it down for others to empty.'

'So they really never come out?'

'No.'

Emma points to one of the biggest trees. Very high up, just under the canopy of leaves, I see four legs dangling over a wooden panel. 'They've been up that tree for over a month.'

'Goodness.'

'Protecting these giants requires commitment.'

'Sounds familiar.'

Emma winks.

The Upper Florentine Valley is a stretch of temperate old-growth rainforest, she explains. Much of it is protected and designated a

World Heritage Site. And the gigantic eucalyptus trees – the largest deciduous trees on earth – also contain a huge amount of carbon, which protects against climate change. And yet Forestry Tasmania has issued Gunns Limited with a licence to cut 50 hectares. The company uses the wood to make toilet paper which it exports to Asia. Some of the trees are more than 400 years old and over 100 metres high.

The sandy road leads to a large open space where several hundred people have gathered. The clearing is full of tree-stumps and abandoned trunks. It's like a graveyard among the giant trees, providing the dancing and singing crowd with some refreshing shade.

Emma has to return to the main road to escort the next group to the meeting place. She wishes us an enjoyable afternoon and disappears off among the trees. Her impish face with the silver nose ring, old dreadlocks and tatty clothes give her an air of intransigence. In a mythical setting she'd be a wood nymph, patron of this magnificent forest. Her unswerving passion is erotic, I can tell from the tingling in my underbelly. Here in the woods, under the tree ferns, on the banks of the Florentine River or in one of the tree huts: for a moment I'm head over heels in love with Emma, as so often happens when I meet a pretty activist who commits herself body and soul to the environment. But in the past year my short-lived romances with activists have proved to be autumn leaves, briefly whipped to great heights by a sensual breeze, but swept into the gutter at the first sign of rain.

Besides, in the past few weeks my thoughts have often wandered to Andrea, who rejected me so ruthlessly in that pub in Rotterdam. Drawing on my rusty detective skills, I managed to track her down on the internet. I refused to take no for an answer. I got in touch and after some pathetic attention seeking on my part we're now emailing practically every day. She's not an activist, far from it, so perhaps we have a future together.

'Fancy a sip?' Crew member Mike hands me a bottle of red wine that's been in chief engineer Larry's rucksack too long. The wine is warm and wouldn't be very nice if it didn't bring a pleasant glow to my cheeks. I can tell from Pete and Larry's flushed faces that they're already halfway through another bottle, so I quickly take a large swig to catch up. The engineer uncorks some more bottles and before the first speaker has even begun, the captain and Larry are messing around on a tree trunk, a little the worse for wear.

Our team is standing at the back of the crowd, on the edge of the forest. The clearing has filled with about 2,000 people eager to make a statement against global warming. The speeches here are the same as conservation speeches all over the world: a neglectful government (Forestry Tasmania), a greedy corporation (Gunns Limited) and an urgent need for a sustainable solution (which is often lacking).

The final speaker concludes by introducing the Australian activist and musician Xavier Rudd. A great admirer of Captain Watson, he mounts the improvised podium in his Sea Shepherd hoodie. The crowd falls silent as soon as he starts strumming his guitar. To the accompaniment of a soft breeze rustling in the enormous eucalyptus trees, he plays the first few bars of 'Better People'.

'People saving whales/And giving your thanks to our seas,' he sings with great emotion. He points to the five black Sea Shepherd Crew shirts who are listening to his performance. Xavier's brief pause is filled by the cheering and clapping crowd in front of us. A couple of people standing nearby turn towards us and yell: 'Go Sea Shepherd. Fuck the Whalers!'

A little gobsmacked, the five of us on the tree trunk nod and wave feebly at the supporters. The artist resumes: 'My respect to the ones in the forest/Standing up for our old trees.' Now he raises a clenched fist at the two activists who've been up in the tree for over a month. The demonstrators start cheering. For several minutes, the two treesitters bask in deafening applause. We join in, clapping twice as hard as anyone else. This was exactly what I needed after the glitter and glamour of the States: the company of grassroots activists who, indifferent to status or fame, throw themselves into a green cause. I can't wait to get back to Antarctica.

Xavier Rudd's performance brings the Walk Against Warming to an end. The demonstrators disperse. Unfortunately the booze proves too much for our chief engineer: he falls off a tree trunk and remains motionless on the ground. 'Broken ribs,' he groans. Mike and I help the South African to his feet, but he turns ashen and collapses. We rush to the nearest hospital, where the news is worse than his self-diagnosis: broken ribs and a punctured lung. Our chief engineer – after the captain the most important person on board – is barred from joining the campaign by the doctor.

The two aborted attempts and the loss of our engineer don't bode well for the Waltzing Matilda campaign. But we ignore the warning signs. The endangered giants of the sea are expecting us.

In June 2013 the wood activists' peaceful protest finally paid off: large parts of the Tasmanian primeval forests, including the Upper Florentine Valley, were designated World Heritage Sites.

26

THE BATMOBILE

It's surprisingly crowded on the Franklin Wharf, a stone's throw from the bustling Salamanca Square and the surrounding shops and cafés. With only a week to go until Christmas, many Tasmanians are stocking up for the holidays. A visit to our futuristic boat makes a pleasant change from the shopping.

'Welcome on board,' I say with a practised smile to a father and his son of about ten who have stopped by the *Ady Gil*. It looks like the mother is staying on the quay.

'Wouldn't you like to come inside?'

'No, I'm fine where I am,' is her firm answer.

I won't press. Behind her is a long queue of people patiently waiting their turn to have a look inside the black crowd puller. I'd better get a move on.

We're lucky to have so many visitors filled with the spirit of Christmas. Virtually every passer-by leaves a little something. Money mostly; sometimes a big sum, usually a couple of dollars.

The donations help us pay our way without having to appeal to the Sea Shepherd headquarters for financial support.

Some visitors ask us what we need, leave with a hastily scribbled list and return a little later with a carrier bag full of fresh fruit, vegetables, vegetarian microwave meals or cartons of soy milk.

Our small fridge is chock-full. Not that it holds much. You'd expect to find an appliance this big in student digs where it would be used to cool a few bottles of lager. And it's not in a proper galley either. Our little kitchen consists of two worktops measuring 1.5 metres by 40 centimetres. One holds a breadmaker, an electric pan and a kettle, which leaves a tiny surface for, say, chopping vegetables. A shelf above the worktop holds a microwave oven, which has been secured with straps. Of the four electrical appliances, we can only use one at a time or else we blow a fuse.

Next to the microwave are several Tupperware boxes and ready-made meals in cardboard packaging. Everything has been fixed with straps and elastic bands. Right now everything is securely on the shelves, but experience has taught us that as soon as the ship starts moving, everything that's not tied down will go flying.

Opposite the first worktop is a second one. This one has a drain and it's where we wash the dishes with seawater while we're travelling. We have to use our drinking water sparingly, because the *Ady Gil* can only store 200 litres. The *Steve Irwin* is a luxury yacht compared to this tiny boat.

From the quay, the father lowers his son onto one of the floats. Our trimaran is in a beautiful spot, but it sits very low in the water when the tide is out. And the absence of a gangplank makes climbing on board a nightmare.

The boy slides effortlessly off the float, walks across a wooden plank to the afterdeck and starts fingering our jet ski. Jimmy, who's cleaning the water scooter, is friendly yet firm as he shoos the little fellow away.

The father clambers onto the float on all fours and hesitates briefly before crossing the wooden plank in two big steps.

'What a bizarre ship,' says the burly Australian as he wipes the sweat from his brow with studied nonchalance.

'Like the Batmobile,' his son adds enthusiastically.

'What are those fins, or horns, on top?'

'Those are the exhausts. They're that high so the ship can pierce the waves. She's been designed to cut through 7-metre waves.'

'So how fast does this thing go?' the visitor asks while touching the inside of the *Ady Gil*.

'Normally 40 knots, but a little less now because we've reinforced the bottom with Kevlar and the prop pitch has been readjusted.'

'Fast enough for the Japs?'

'Fast enough to catch up with the harpoon vessels.'

'Aren't you afraid of the ice?'

As soon as the visitors realise they only have a couple of minutes, the questions come thick and fast.

'Scared stiff.'

'Seriously?'

'Yes, the ship is made of carbon-fibre, which is extremely hard-wearing, but very fragile. If we hit ice, we've had it. Hence the extra Kevlar.'

'What kind of engine do you have?'

'Twin 540 horsepower Cummins Mercruiser,' answers Pete as he squeezes past with a toolbox. He stops and poses for a photo with the little boy.

'I set the world record for circumnavigating the globe in a biodiesel-powered vessel with this boat. Sixty days. Now we're using it to save whales.' The captain beams.

'How many of you are there?'

'There are five of us this time.'

The tour takes us to the back of the trimaran. 'This door on the right leads to the engine room, on the left we've got the toilet.'

The man opens the door and sees a toilet bowl bolted to the deck. Toilet rolls, deck swabbers, brooms and cleaning materials fill the rest of the space. He enters the cubicle.

'There's literally not enough room to swing a cat in here. How on earth do you wipe your ass?'

'Better not think about it,' I tell him, amused.

'How do you shower?'

'There's no shower on board.'

His dubious mien turns completely incredulous.

'How long will you be away?'

'Until March if we have to, almost three months. Supplies come from the *Steve Irwin*.'

'Incredible.'

He's quiet as he takes in the claustrophobic space. His son's not bothered by the discomforts; he wants to come along. He has clambered onto one of the two bright green racing seats (our only chairs) and yanks hard at the helm.

'Stay where you are.' Dad photographs the kid in various poses and with silly faces.

'You're a proper captain now,' I'm selling our attraction like a funfair operator who'll do anything for a bit of cash.

'What's this?' the boy replies.

'GPS. We use it to determine our position.'

'And this?'

'Radar.'

'And this?'

'Fuel gauge.' I reckon the answers matter bugger all.

'This?'

'Radio.'

'Why are the seats green?'

'No idea. The captain's favourite colour,' I fib.

'Oh. How about this?'

'The gearbox.'

The father is taking great pride in his little smarty pants, and I answer his childish questions with unflagging zeal. After umpteen of them, his dad finally calls it a day, saying mum is waiting. To conclude, there's the sleeping area. Four beds attached to the wall in the tip of the boat. They're like hammocks.

'We're hot bunking. Two guys are always up, while the rest are asleep. When you wake up you give up your bed to the person whose turn it is to sleep.'

'No emergency exit?' the man notes.

'No, if we capsize, we can only get out by hacking a hole with an axe that's kept in the tip of the boat.'

'You guys are super cool,' the little fellow shouts.

'Crazy stuff,' his old man concludes matter-of-factly.

'If you work really hard in school you too can become a Sea Shepherd when you grow up.'

A bit of pedagogical nonsense that always goes down well with the parents.

'Absolutely.' Dad gives the lad a pat on the head and nudges him gently towards the exit at the back of the ship.

'Cool. I want to do this too. Can I come along?'

'Yeah, sure, when you're 18.'

Outside, dad hoists the little guy up with a laugh and plants his feet on the quay. The boy rushes over to his mother and launches into an incoherent story.

The father turns round. 'Let me shake your hand.' He squeezes hard. 'The very best of luck. What you guys are doing is both brave and insane. But someone's got to stop those Japs. I really admire you. I couldn't do it myself. Best of luck.' He hands me a $20 note. 'Thanks for the tour.'

'Thank you, and thanks for stopping by.'

'No worries.'

'Welcome to the *Ady Gil*,' I greet the next couple of visitors. There are at least 50 people waiting, and it's still early. I heave a sigh.

Mike, who's just escorting his visitor out, sighs too. Pete sticks his head out of the stairwell by the rear exit and spots the long queue. Grinning broadly, the skipper shakes his head. This is going to be a very long final day in Hobart.

27

THE GILBILLIES

So far the crossing to Antarctica has been all plain sailing. Long, rolling billows are pushing the *Ady Gil* southwards. Every so often a gentle wave lifts our vessel out of the water and lets it surf the crest for a few seconds. Not only does it feel good, but it also allows us to travel at an average speed of 14 knots without using up too much fuel.

Three days into the expedition, the fledgling whale savers are slowly getting used to life at sea. The only one still reeling with nausea is our new crew member Jason. The captain called him up at the last minute to replace the injured first engineer. Jason is familiar with the engines as he was part of the crew back when the ship was still known as *Earthrace*. Even so, his first few hours at sea are always marred by seasickness.

Captain Bethune wastes no time setting out the ship's hierarchy: 'When I drop out, Laurens will be in charge. When he's lost, Mike will assume command.'

'And as soon as Mike's out cold too, there'll be just the two of you,' Pete chortles, 'and you'll have to save your own skin.'

Then he starts allocating the jobs. I'm responsible for communication with headquarters. We're also each assigned a shift at the helm and we have to take turns cooking.

After the short briefing it's a question of getting used to this whirling washing machine and the accent of my fellow passengers. The four New Zealanders chew on each and every word and swallow most of it before spitting out an incomprehensible pulp through pursed lips. And they talk non-stop.

Pete and Jason have an opinion about absolutely everything and seem to be producing sound even when they're not actually saying anything. In the opposite corner are Mike and Jimmy. The first thing you notice about Mike, a firefighter, is his calm demeanour. His bald pate, with folds of skin virtually covering his gentle eyes, and his burly physique make him the ship's Big Friendly Giant. Jimmy on the other hand is Tom Thumb. Short, but absolutely fearless. The former navy diver throws himself into every job he's asked to do and usually responds drily in sentences of little more than two words.

As a Dutchman, I'm the foreigner on the New Zealand ship. Pete didn't really want me on board. The skipper wanted to work with his own people. But my campaign experience and pressure from headquarters brought the captain round in the end. After a couple of days Pete's misgivings are all but gone. He treats me the same as the rest of the group, although as the orange among kiwis I'll always be the odd one out.

But if truth be told, all five of us are curious characters in the Sea Shepherd legion and we're sailing a perilous ocean in a minuscule boat. And we're on a mission: we're going into battle, armed with bow and arrow, butyric acid and a spud gun. We're the gadflies intent on making life hell for the *Nisshin Maru* and the harpoon vessels. One small vessel against the immense whaling fleet. Before long the nickname the Ady Gilbillies is born.

Mike's in his hammock, reading a book. Jimmy's lying underneath with a laptop. The first couple of days he occasionally passed the laptop round to share a smutty porn clip. It didn't last: five guys packed into tight quarters have little use for sexual stimulation.

In the galley Jason is stir-frying the last of our fresh vegetables. He makes them go further by adding soy sausage. On this vessel we're trying, Sea-Shepherd style, to cater to a vegan diet. Every hot meal is effectively a stir-fry because we only have one pan. But each dish is given its own name.

We take turns cooking. As it was on the other vessels, dinner's one of the highlights of the day; perhaps even more so on the *Ady Gil*. The aroma of Jason's vegetable dish briefly dispels the diesel fumes that are a constant on the ship. There's not much we can do about ventilation. The cockpit is completely enclosed. Only the pilothouse has a tiny sliding window that lets in fresh air.

Jason fills each of the bowls and passes them round. We wolf our portion down. Dinner is always a hurried affair: one wave and your plate goes flying. I wash down the last few bites with a cup of hot tea. Jason slips out and returns a couple of seconds later with a bucket of seawater: for he who does the cooking also does the washing-up (forcing the chef to make less of a mess).

After dinner, I retrieve the latest emails via our satellite connection. The laptop and sat phone are our only link with the outside world. I write an email to Andrea, who's following our expedition closely. Our emails began with short, friendly exchanges, but are gradually turning into love letters. Not knowing when we'll see each other again allows us to write without any fear or inhibitions. As we bare our souls we fall in love without actually staring into each other's eyes.

When the emails are done, I start plotting a route towards the *Steve Irwin*, with which we're having a rendezvous tonight. The Japanese security vessel *Shonan Maru No. 2* has been bearing down on our flagship for days and is preventing the *Steve* from getting closer to the whaling fleet. Captain Watson wants us to intervene.

The skipper is at the helm. He's got one leg pulled up under him and one foot resting on the dashboard. Pete pulls a teabag out of a large mug and puts it down next to a large collection of used bags in the corner of the armrest. When no one's talking to him he tends to have a faraway look on his face. I find it difficult to get a handle on Pete. His seamanship is not in doubt. I've never felt unsafe under his command. But whenever he talks about whaling, his expression changes. He will screw up his beady eyes and tilt his head a little. Sometimes the captain will whisper, as though our trip has a secret mission. The New Zealander believes Sea Shepherd is too nice to the whalers. And while he knows he's under Watson's command, he has his own take on things. We have a longbow on board, for example, and arrows dipped in a chemical substance.

'As soon as they kill a whale, I'll shoot an arrow into the animal. The Japanese won't be able to sell it when they see it's been poisoned.'

A peculiar plan, to say the least.

He's extremely fidgety. And he keeps coming up with yet more plans of attack. In between his sentences he'll sneak sly glances at the ocean to see if anyone's around. The more he talks about his plans, the more I realise that the skipper is desperate to prove himself.

'We've got meat hooks on board. So when they've got a whale on deck, Mike can drop me off with the jet ski and I'll use the hooks to climb up. They'll have no choice but to haul me on board the *Nisshin Maru*. Imagine the loss of face for the Japanese.' The daredevil sips his tea, convinced his idea is brilliant.

'Those water cannons are incredibly powerful. You'll never pull it off,' I challenge him.

'That's because you guys didn't do it properly. Sea Shepherd has been far too meek in recent years. It's time to show some balls.

That's what we're here for. We're not going to throw stinkbombs, we're going to fight.'

Pete's self-assurance verges on misplaced arrogance. After two Antarctica campaigns I know how hard it is to fight the fleet without violence. I hope the captain won't cross that boundary. But then that's precisely why the Sea Shepherd director asked me to join the team: to keep an eye on the skipper.

'Hmm, hmm.' I don't fancy a discussion.

'I'd jump on board a harpoon vessel any day,' he resumes.

'Me too!' shouts Jimmy, who's listening with half an ear.

'Let's all do it, Jimmy, so they'll have to take everybody back to Japan,' Pete laughs.

'It's been done before. I don't know if there's much point in jumping on board. As far as I'm aware they arrest you and take you to Japan. That's all.'

'It would put a stop to the hunt.'

'How's that?'

'The international loss of face, the shame of an activist climbing on board. It would be a scandal in Japan. It would put whaling in the spotlight over there.'

'I doubt it.'

I don't want to sound too pessimistic, but after two campaigns I no longer believe that a single action can stop the hunt. The only thing that works is blocking the *Nisshin*'s slipway.

'We'll see.'

Something about the way he says those words makes me feel uneasy. Pete has a volatile aura. Our captain screws up his eyes again and stares outside. A sinister little laugh steals over his face. He's hatching a plan without consulting anyone. I do admire his guts though. After all, he sailed the globe in this boat, weathered mighty storms and set a world record, but when he talks about stopping the whale hunt he sounds fearless. And that worries me: if you're fearless you don't stop to think.

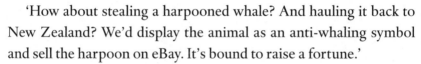

'How about stealing a harpooned whale? And hauling it back to New Zealand? We'd display the animal as an anti-whaling symbol and sell the harpoon on eBay. It's bound to raise a fortune.'

'Sure, Pete.'

'Yeah, that would be really cool.'

28

BAZOOKAS AND LASERS

23 December 2009, 00.30 hours
Position: 61° 57' S, 153° 185' E
Fuel: 7,750 litres
Water: 150 litres

The radar-repellent anti-slip paint in which the *Ady Gil* has been dipped is effective: the *Steve Irwin* doesn't notice us in the twilight until we're actually visible to the naked eye. The ship's lighting is off because we want to keep our presence a surprise to the Japanese security vessel that's sailing 7 miles away. Without slowing down and arousing suspicions, our flagship launches a rubber boat to pick us up.

Pete and I are waiting on the stern in our black drysuits and life jackets. We look like commandos and I'm not exaggerating. Our captain likes the militaristic look. Back in Hobart he told us to shave our heads and now these special-forces outfits complete the picture.

The Delta team picks us up and carries us to the *Steve Irwin*. On board we're immediately taken to Captain Watson. On our way I hug a couple of crew members I know from previous campaigns. Inside I get a whiff of the boat's unmistakable smell: it's like perfume to a sea conservationist.

Our meeting with the captain is a short one. Our mission is simple: Watson wants us to harass the *Shonan Maru No. 2* for as long as we can. We're given a prop fouler to do the job.

Pete remarks that the ropes don't usually work. It's still a deterrent, Watson counters. While we're busy holding up the security vessel, the *Irwin* will try to bridge the thirty-odd miles it needs to move out of radar range. Captain Watson gives us a set of handheld lasers. Although they're harmless, the bright beams may irritate the helmsman on the Japanese vessel. Lastly, Watson asks if we want to take a shower. It would appear that our solitary confinement in the airless catacombs of the *Ady Gil* has enveloped us in an almost unbearable odour. The pilothouse has begun to smell of unwashed socks and stale male sweat.

'If the rest of the crew can't shower, we won't either,' Pete and I say. 'But we wouldn't mind a cup of hot chocolate,' the skipper adds. We walk over to the mess, where the table is littered with some of the leftovers from dinner. Baked sweet potatoes, quinoa and fresh vegetables tantalise our taste buds after the frugal meals on the *Ady Gil*. Having already put out some cake for us, the ship's cook is now filling a bag with chocolate bars for the rest of our crew. We quickly pour the hot chocolate down our throats and chase it down with a soft drink, something we've been craving for ages. And while going through our tactics one last time, we devour a final piece of cake. After these delicious snacks, we hug the cook and return to the rubber boat.

Just before we set off, Simeon Houtman comes running. That's right, we almost forgot: Animal Planet promised us a cameraman once we made it to Antarctica. He's lugging a backpack and a suitcase full of equipment. Simeon is reluctant. The producer assures him that it's just for the action against the *Shonan Maru*. When it's over, we'll return Simeon to the *Irwin* and get someone else from the *Bob Barker*. It seems to set the cameraman's mind at ease.

The Delta drops us off at the *Ady Gil*, and as soon as the prop fouler is transferred our boat sails away from the Sea Shepherd flagship like a thief in the night, en route to the *Shonan Maru No. 2*.

The *Ady Gil* drifts in the *Irwin*'s wake in the hope that the security vessel doesn't spot us and will head in our direction of its own accord.

'OK, boys,' Pete yells. 'We're going to do some damage. Get ready, Jimmy, you're firing the spud gun.' He retrieves the potato pistol from the front hold. With its black duct tape and sight, the spud gun looks like a bazooka, but all it does is fire potatoes, apples or maybe butyric acid using air pressure. Since the *Nisshin Maru*'s nets were unassailable last year, we're hoping that this time round our secret weapon can land the rancid butter on deck.

'Mike, you're in charge of the prop fouler. You decide how to launch it. Jason, you're staying in the cockpit to provide assistance where necessary. Laurens, you've done all this before, so you can coach Mike and Jimmy and take pictures. Simeon, it's up to you how and what to film, as long as you don't get in anyone's way.' The nervous cameraman is receiving a crash course in adjustment. In what little time is left, he tries to get his equipment ready.

Mike stomps outside, a cap pulled down over his ears and a drysuit over his thermal underwear. Jimmy follows him, carrying the 'spud gun from hell', as Pete likes to call the thing. He attaches the air hose to the compressor in the engine room. I prepare a basket with apples and rotten potatoes for the navy diver. And I take pictures wherever I go. Simeon, who's keen to get his shots in too, regularly digs me in the ribs. Together we shuffle across the afterdeck, which is far too small for four people.

Mike has suspended the prop fouler with a clever rope construction that slides into the water via the floats at the stern.

He's hoping to launch the prop fouler at the right time with a quick release pin, a hook and a piece of rope. Jason is in the kitchen as a go-between, passing our messages on to Pete.

We're all ready when the *Shonan Maru* approaches. Although we're just a few hundred metres away, the Japanese captain still doesn't notice us. Pete accelerates and charges at the whaling vessel. Now the ship spots us and reacts with a sharp turn to starboard. It speeds away at more than 20 knots.

They've only ever seen the *Ady Gil* in newspapers and now it suddenly looms before them. Shocked, the whalers leave the battlefield. Pete gives chase to show the *Shonan Maru* that we're faster. The Japanese flee, and after a couple of miles the *Steve Irwin*'s first mate calls me to say that our strategy is working: the distance between them is now 11 miles and steadily increasing. If we can keep it up, the *Irwin* will escape. But no sooner has the officer hung up than the *Shonan* changes course. The Japanese vessel performs a flanking manoeuvre, but it looks like she's heading back towards the *Steve Irwin*.

'Here we go,' Pete yells. Jason relays the message loudly. 'Jimmy first!' The *Ady Gil* now sails alongside the *Shonan Maru*. There's nobody on deck. The whalers don't know what the deal is with this futuristic boat. And although the LRAD sonic cannon can be heard, with shrill beeping fanning out across the sea, it doesn't bother us.

'You see the LRAD? Aim for that or else the radar. It's OK to hit equipment, but ab-so-lute-ly no people. You get that?' I repeat my question and wait for Jimmy to answer in the affirmative. We mustn't injure anyone. It would be a blot on Sea Shepherd's reputation and a PR disaster.

'Go for it.' Jimmy aims the airgun at the harpoon vessel and fires. The first apple overshoots the ship by a ridiculous margin. 'Keep trying,' I encourage him. 'It was the right direction!' We have to shout at the top of our lungs in order to be heard over the LRAD and the roaring engines of the *Ady Gil*.

Meanwhile Mike has picked up a laser and flashes it at the bridge of the *Shonan Maru*. The ship veers away again. But not for long, because the whalers soon realise that the green light beam doesn't do anything. They're back on a course that will take them to the *Steve Irwin*. But our marksman is getting into the swing of things and is happily firing away. Reloading is becoming easier and one after the other, rotten vegetables go flying towards the Japanese vessel. That said, Jimmy keeps narrowly missing the radar, so the *Shonan* stays on course. We reckon that while we're obstructing and delaying the vessel, the *Steve Irwin* can increase its distance, but over the phone we learn that it's slow going. Time for the prop fouler.

Mike is sitting on the stern, holding the quick release rope in his hands. He signals that he's ready. The *Ady Gil* accelerates and the rope quickly whips past the bow of the *Shonan Maru*. Mike yanks hard at the quick-release mechanism, but then the rope snaps and we're still trailing the prop fouler behind us. A miss.

The firefighter from New Zealand decides to do a manual launch. Within minutes he has wound one end of the prop fouler around a rail and is holding the tail end, his feet braced against the rear of the *Ady Gil*. I go inside to tell Pete to take the bend a bit wider. The captain is bare-chested at the helm now, his body glistening with sweat, which accentuates the Maori tattoos covering his body. He's grinning from ear to ear. 'This is terrific. But God almighty it's nerve-racking to sail in front of that big ship. And I can see fuck all through these tiny windows.'

'You're doing really well... so far,' I add, amused.

'Ready for the second round?'

'Let's go.'

I go back outside. We try again. Mike is so nervous he releases the prop fouler too soon. The rope disappears, but not around the *Shonan Maru*'s propeller. Another miss. While we try and recover it the Japanese security vessel increases its distance by a couple of miles and gets the *Steve Irwin* in its sights again. Our cool boat may be faster, but for now there's little we can do about the harpoon vessels. First we need some decent practice with the prop fouler.

The first mate is on the line. His message: we failed. There's no point carrying on. We receive new coordinates and are told to proceed towards the factory ship *Nisshin Maru*. Now that we know our limitations, the team refocuses on the mission for which the fast trimaran was bought in the first place: to locate the whaling fleet as quickly as possible.

Disappointed, we take stock: prop fouling disastrous, spud gun great, collaboration OK. And hey, we're still afloat. But my camera is kaput. Animal Planet forgot to pack a water cover and the salt water has ruined the lens. I proceed to upload the handful of photos that have come out all right to our headquarters in Friday Harbor. A couple of hours later the whole world is up to speed on our first action.

Exhausted by the strain, we all hit the sack. The cameraman improvises a berth on the ground, in between the beds. Five of us go to sleep, while Jimmy's the first to keep watch. Four hours later I relieve him. He's nodding off at the helm, barely aware that he's being relieved. Without a word, he rolls off the chair and into my warm bed. A few hours later the captain packs me off to bed.

After forty winks, the crew wakes up to a delicious smell. The skipper is baking pancakes with our last bit of batter. We spread a thin layer of jam on them and scoff the lot. Morale goes through the stomach, because along with the pancakes our disappointment vanishes. We conclude that our action was a more or less successful exercise and that we're now ready for the real thing.

The *Steve Irwin* has no other choice but to head back to Australia's territorial waters to shake off its pursuers. For us, refuelling or resupplying is out of the question for the foreseeable future. Support will come from our other ship, the *Bob Barker*. But she's 1,600 sea miles away, held up by a terrible storm. The *Ady Gil* is all alone here in Antarctica, slowly setting course for the south, without wasting fuel. Our shelves are emptying, our water supply is dwindling fast and assistance is thousands of kilometres away. Mike's none too pleased.

29

THE CALM BEFORE THE DEVASTATING STORM

It's Christmas Day. The whalers are nowhere to be seen. And we're still waiting for new coordinates from headquarters. Pete has reduced our speed to 6 knots per hour, so we're only using 150 litres of fuel a day. We need to take it easy in case we get another chance to stop the *Nisshin Maru*. Or to simply keep going. There are only 6,300 litres left in the tank and at top speed the engines burn up 100 litres per hour.

We can refuel via the *Bob Barker*, which is carrying several hundred tons of fuel, but the Sea Shepherd vessel is a ten-day journey away. Maybe more if the storm they're in persists. If assistance isn't forthcoming we'll have to sail back to Hobart or New Zealand – a scenario none of us is keen on, except Mike. He's expected back at the fire station shortly, but it looks like we won't see the mainland anytime soon. The firefighter feels screwed, because Pete had promised to get him back in time. Our chief engineer has other commitments too, but seems less bothered by the delay. Mike, on the other hand, is growing more cantankerous by the day. The burly New Zealander retires to the afterdeck more often and participates less in conversations. The only thing on which he expresses his increasingly irate views is our dwindling water supply.

'Just over 100 litres left,' he grumbles.

'Don't worry,' the captain says, a little irritably. Every day now starts with a tiresome remark about water. Mike does some quick calculations: 'Six guys times a minimum of 2 litres of water a day, that gives us less than nine days. The *Bob Barker* is a ten-day journey away. We need water to survive.'

'Don't panic,' Pete now says laconically. When Mike's not looking, he rolls his eyes. The skipper is trying to reassure Mike. Nobody wants to antagonise the almost 2-metre tall giant and see him stomping around the ship. Although on good days he's known for his great sense of humour, on bad days like today he is consumed by worries. His motivation dissipates with every disappearing litre of water. And on a tiny ship like this we can't afford to lose anyone, let alone waste energy on keeping our crew in check.

'Mike, we're sailing around the biggest fresh water reservoir in the world,' I explain patronisingly. 'If we run out of water, we'll just collect some ice. Problem solved.'

The firefighter considers my suggestion and seems to accept it. He makes his way to the afterdeck to be alone.

'If a problem can be fixed, there's no need to worry. If a problem can't be fixed, there's no point in worrying,' I say cheerfully.

There are question marks in Pete's eyes, guessing at the origins of this unexpected wisdom. 'A Buddhist saying.'

The captain ponders these words and says: 'I'm going to check on the food.'

Pete is off to the engine room, where his tofurkey (turkey-style tofu), potatoes and vegetables are roasting on the engine blocks.

The foil-wrapped food has been there all day and the cook is hoping it's finally done. He's back soon and declares it more or less edible.

That's the cue for me to prepare the gravy. The recipe, from one of the vegan cookbooks on board, calls for fresh mushrooms, but those were gone after two days at sea. The only thing vaguely reminiscent of mushrooms is the smell of fungus that fills your nostrils when you enter the boat. I'll have to improvise.

'Dinner time,' Pete announces loudly. It's the best time of the day. Simeon switches his camera off and squeezes between Mike and Jason, who are sitting on one of the beds. The plates are passed round. The tofu and potatoes are drenched in the gravy, so the bone-dry spuds don't stick to the roof of your mouth for all eternity. The captain conjures up a bottle of whisky. It's the only alcohol on board, donated by a generous soul in Hobart. 'Enjoy. When it's gone it's gone.'

We nurse our mugs as if it's the last booze on earth. We take small sips. The warming liquid enters my bloodstream immediately, tickling every vein along the way. I've seen these men pour pint after pint down their throats on ordinary weekday nights, but now, after only a couple of sips, their cheeks flush and they're giggling like school boys at silly, mostly food-related jokes. With the exception of the cameraman, all four miss a bit of meat with their meagre serving of vegetables.

Anecdotes about culinary feasts follow. They shift our thoughts to families thousands of kilometres away, gathered round the tree and raising their glass to a merry Christmas. The poignant memories and the alcohol produce an emotionally charged silence in which each of us thinks of the family we've left behind for this journey. Are we selfish because we've opted for adventure and abandoned our loved ones? Or are we noble for choosing the whales over and above a cosy Christmas? Am I trying to change the world for the better or am I simply an adventurer? What's preferable: loyalty to your family and always being there for them, or going out into the world to fight wrongs whatever the cost?

I've now been away from the Netherlands for almost three years, and on special occasions such as today I miss my family more than ever. But the final sip of whisky washes all thoughts of home away.

Mike fills a bucket with seawater for the dishes, while the captain takes the helm for his shift, the engineer checks the engines for the last time today, Jimmy makes tea for whoever wants some, and Simeon picks up his camera and interviews Pete for the umpteenth time, asking the same old questions. I crawl into my sleeping bag and try to get some sleep. I want to drift off to dreamland, thinking of everything that makes the Netherlands so beautiful.

We're moving at a snail's pace across the vast expanse of sea. December 26, 27, 28 and 29 pass uneventfully. The days are long and dull and I fill them with lengthy declarations of love to Andrea.

Without new coordinates, we sail around in a search pattern of our own invention. Every now and then we hear a shrill squawk over the radio, but no Japanese voices. We have a sneaking suspicion that the whalers are nearby but haven't got the faintest idea where.

The *Ady Gil* has only 4,500 litres of fuel and 50 litres of water left.

Then it's 30 December. Snow whirls gracefully around the *Ady Gil* and the water is mirror-smooth. Icebergs force us to navigate carefully. We're sailing gently through the Antarctic waters at 2 knots. Whenever we pass ribbons of mist we stop the engines so as not to bump into any ice.

'Oh my God!' My voice is about four octaves higher than usual. Luckily the others don't notice, as they're just as ecstatic as I am. Three humpbacks are swimming alongside our vessel. At first they seem to be passing, but then they turn round and come back. Two large specimens and a smaller one. One of the big ones, a giant well over 20 metres, rolls onto its back and slaps a pectoral fin on the water as a goodbye wave. We can almost touch the gorgeous animals. Jason whispers: 'This is why we're doing it.' The cameraman almost tumbles into the water while trying to get as close as possible for a

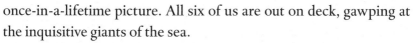

once-in-a-lifetime picture. All six of us are out on deck, gawping at the inquisitive giants of the sea.

With imperial dignity their backs emerge out of the water so they can breathe. A ferocious gust of air blasts across Antarctica. Their tailfins are the last to slide back into the depths. Only a ripple on the water remains.

Suddenly the biggest one resurfaces. It looks at me, or at least that's what I think. Whales are cross-eyed. For all I know it's ignoring me completely, but I feel special all the same. The humpback scrutinises me, the crew and our ship before disappearing under water. After several dozen metres, it comes up for air again. The two other whales follow and together they move on. I quietly thank the animals for making an appearance. We hope that one day the humpbacks – the composers of the sea – will sing a song about that peculiar black ship and its crew, if only not to be forgotten.

31 December
Postion: 64° 09' S, 149° 34' E
Fuel: 3,800 litres
Water: 30 litres

The minutes are ticking away slowly. That's to say, the bright, fluorescent red numbers on the dashboard are slow to change. It's almost midnight. The wind is raw and waves wash over the roof of our ship. We're imprisoned in the hold of the *Ady Gil*, unable to go out. Our mugs are filled with tea instead of champagne. The treats brought out to celebrate New Year's Eve consist of a bar of chocolate, biscuits and dried fruit.

The crew have gathered in the pilothouse. We're staring into space or through the tiny windows at the drops of water rolling down forlornly. None of us is dressed for a festive evening. On the contrary. We've been wearing the same clothes for weeks on end, at least indoors: thermal underwear and over that sometimes a pair of trousers or a jumper.

It's five to twelve. We all write our wishes on scraps of paper, which the captain then stuffs into the empty whisky bottle. At midnight, we propose a toast. 'Cheers. Happy New Year.' Pete ushers in the year: 'It's a great privilege to be sailing around Antarctica with this team.' We raise our mugs in agreement.

'What next?' Mike asks when nobody follows this with anything sensible. We look at each other, not knowing what to do or say.

'Nothing,' I finally offer. 'That was it.'

'Happy New Year,' Jimmy yells drily. 'Awesome party.' We all burst out laughing. 'Best New Year ever,' the skipper jokes. He walks to the back door and tosses the bottled wishes into the sea. The rest of us go to bed.

The next day, the sea is still inhospitable. Our water situation is getting precarious; we only have 20 litres left in the jerrycans. Mike reckons we really ought to start looking for water and says so more firmly than ever. Mutiny seems imminent. Pete promises to go fishing for a piece of ice as soon as the weather allows.

Every once in a while our radio produces static. We still believe that the whalers are close by. No new instructions from Captain Watson. We persist with our own search pattern.

Around noon, when the sky temporarily clears, Mike and I fish a chunk of ice out of the water. There's no iceberg in sight, so the chunk must have been floating in the water for weeks. I hack a piece off it and taste it. Salty! The ice is far too porous and has absorbed seawater. Tomorrow we'll look for a proper iceberg, the skipper promises.

For dinner that evening I prepare what I've dubbed farmhouse curry, an improvised recipe using a tin of kidney beans, chickpeas and a microwave meal that's supposed to be Indian. The crew shovel the frugal meal into their mouths, albeit with visible reluctance. They've got no choice; it's all we've got.

It's 2 January. We've got 10 litres of water left. The sun is burning a hole in the cloud cover and urges the wind to die down. The *Ady Gil* is bobbing gently beside a pristine white iceberg. Swimming pool-blue waves wash over the base. On one side, waves have carved a natural slide. Pete and Jimmy are in their drysuits, ready to dive in and swim towards the berg.

'If we catch an incoming wave and wash onto that slide, we can use the meat hooks to climb on top of the iceberg,' the skipper reckons. Jimmy nods like an obedient, disciplined soldier, eager to do his job. They attach a security rope and jump into the icy water. With a few jerrycans trailing behind them, they swim to the iceberg. And lo and behold, Pete's plan is working. The swell pushes the swimmers up and, after a couple of failed attempts, they manage to pull themselves up with the hooks. The ice collectors do a little victory dance on top of the berg. Jimmy hacks his meat hook into the ice to hew some chunks off. The tip is blunted with each blow, but the surface refuses to crack. The ice, which could well be centuries old, is far too hard. Both men slide back down into the water. And again. It's far too much fun to swim straight back.

Floating at the foot of the iceberg are some chunks that have calved off. The two swimmers haul some of them back to the *Ady Gil*. This time it's fresh water. I'm busy until the early hours of the morning, melting the ice in the microwave and funnelling it into the jerrycans. We managed to collect 60 litres of water, enough to hold out until our supply ship arrives.

I've had it up to here. The nasty food, the cramped quarters, the stench, the same old faces and the long days when nothing happens are eating away at my morale. Besides, I'm regularly woken up by phone calls from headquarters asking for media interviews or campaign updates.

I spend a good part of the day in silence, frequently slipping out with a cup of tea. On the roof of the *Ady Gil*, with my back against the large fins, I peer through binoculars, searching for the whalers and enjoying the calm. When I go back in I'm in much better spirits: the scenery in Antarctica is homeopathic Prozac.

I start doing the dishes. One of the things I've discovered during this trip is that the prevention of insanity is inextricably linked to the attention you lavish on everything you do. And so it's with dedication that I wash each fork, clean the spoons and scrub the pan until every last bit of encrusted food is gone before carefully putting everything away again. The crew members are each handed a mug of tea. Finally I pour myself a mug and take mindful sips. Then I prepare some food for the crew. I'm still sick and tired of the expedition, but at least the day has passed lovingly. Minutes become more bearable when they're lived with conscious awareness.

The next day. 'Guys, who was the last to go before me?' No answer. No surprise there. The perpetrator knows what this is about, the others have their suspicions: a big turd is floating in our tiny toilet bowl. It's covered by a few sheets of toilet paper, but the dark-brown contours are clearly visible.

My gaze flits to Jason, who says in all innocence: 'It wasn't me, honest.' He laughs sheepishly. The same reaction from the rest, including Mike, whom I wake up and subject to a cross-examination.

'Whoever blocked the toilet has to unblock it,' Pete orders. Nobody reacts. 'In that case it's you, Laurens.'

'What!? Piss off, I'm the one who needs to crap. It definitely wasn't me.'

'You discovered it, so if you want to crap you're going to have to fix it.'

'That's really fucked up.'

'Either that or you don't crap.'

'Fucking bastards.' Five men laugh, one just a little louder than the others, but I can't make out which one.

With the greatest possible reluctance, I unscrew the bolts from the bowl, dismantle the drainpipe and gingerly carry the whole thing outside. On the afterdeck I chuck the contents of the toilet bowl into

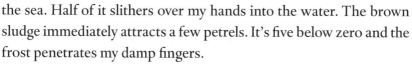

the sea. Half of it slithers over my hands into the water. The brown sludge immediately attracts a few petrels. It's five below zero and the frost penetrates my damp fingers.

The small shredder engine needs to be taken apart. The cogwheels are full of paper and bits of shit. The screws and bolts are so tiny I have to do it with my bare fingers. Every five minutes, I hurry back inside to warm my hands and to have another go at the crew.

The warmly dressed cameraman comes out and films me as I'm picking the half-digested stomach contents of our crew from between the cogwheels while trying not to retch. 'If this isn't going to be an Animal Planet special, I'll eat my camera.' He thinks his remark is witty. I think I hate him right now.

After two hours of fiddling in the cold, our shit box is back in its old place. After I've been, I assure the others that 'they can all crap to their heart's content again'. The loud cheers of those who stood by and watched fill the *Ady Gil*. For the rest of the day, I seek refuge in a book. Yesterday I felt like an enlightened Zen master. Today everybody can drop dead as far as I'm concerned.

On 5 January we get the captain of the *Bob Barker* on the line. He finally has some news, very good news in fact. An Antarctic cruise ship, the *Orion*, unexpectedly came across the entire Japanese whaling fleet. The commander immediately informed Sea Shepherd. Right now, the *Bob Barker* is steaming towards their last known location. We are to head that way too. This is the news we were all dying to hear. Our tank is almost empty and we've nearly run out of food and water, but we're so keen to screw the *Nisshin Maru* that we instantly forget our woes. Everybody's beaming: we finally get to take action. 'We're on our way!' Our skipper puts the helm over and sets course for the *Bob Barker*.

A couple of hours later the captain calls again. They've found the *Nisshin Maru*. The Japanese mother ship is fleeing, but Sea Shepherd has it in her sights!

30

RAMMED!

On 6 January, shortly after midnight, we catch our first glimpse of the factory ship.

'We can see the *Nisshin*,' I communicate to the *Bob Barker* – still just a speck on the horizon. Our new acquisition is making her debut on the battlefield. The former whaler has been converted into a Sea Shepherd vessel and is strong enough to withstand ice. And the 500 tonnes of diesel she's carrying allows her to spend months at sea.

'Can you guys slow down the *Nisshin*? We can't keep up with her,' the captain asks over the ship's telephone. Since she's chock-full of fuel, the *Bob Barker* can't achieve the necessary speed of 16 knots.

'We'll do our best,' Pete replies. The *Ady Gil* is running on her last drops of diesel. We probably only have one chance to attack the *Nisshin Maru* before our expedition comes to a temporary halt. No more fuel and no more food – we'll have to crawl back to the *Steve Irwin*, which thankfully is on her way.

The *Nisshin Maru* is alone at the moment, but the *Bob Barker* reports that the harpoon vessels are approaching. We'd rather not think about it. Right now we're staring at the colossus in front of us.

'Look at that monster…' Jimmy gawks open-mouthed at the gigantic whaler.

'This is the ship that hacks the whales to pieces. Shut this one down and you shut down whaling,' I explain.

'We'd better do our best then,' our marksman says as he slings the spud gun over his shoulder with a broad grin on his face.

Mike is ready with the prop fouler, while Pete is at the helm and Jason acts as our go-between, passing along any messages. The cameraman is scurrying back and forth between the stern and the cockpit to single-handedly capture everything on film. I'm responsible for communications and providing assistance where necessary.

The captain crosses in front of the *Nisshin Maru* a couple of times to see what it feels like. After a couple of practice runs he's ready to obstruct the impressive 8,000 tonne ship for real.

Jason gives us the green light. While Pete manoeuvres alongside, Jimmy fires a couple of rotten potatoes at the whaler's communication dish. These are followed by bottles of butyric acid, which are now easily sailing over the netting.

Pete whizzes past the *Nisshin Maru*. When he yanks the wheel to the right the *Ady Gil* cuts sharply across the bow. Mike is now just a couple of metres from the bow. The factory ship hurtles straight on, its horn blaring loudly. Somewhere in the distance we hear a mechanical-sounding voice telling us to stop immediately. The sonic cannon on the Japanese deck scatters in the wind. Mike lets go of the rope, and the second the prop fouler unravels in the water, Pete accelerates and the *Ady Gil* is off. The factory ship sails over the rope. While under no illusion that we can actually foul the *Nisshin*'s prop, we'll consider our action a success if we manage to delay her just a little.

The *Ady Gil* positions itself behind the *Nisshin Maru*. The prop fouler is nowhere to be seen. We remain in place until the whaler grinds to a halt. Slightly stunned, we stare at the gigantic ocean steamer that is now motionless in the water – all because of our little piece of string.

'*Bob Barker*, the *Nisshin Maru* is dead in the water.'

Cheering on both ships, but I quickly dampen the enthusiasm because it's happened before. Still, the whaler stays put for now, allowing the *Bob Barker* to close in. The harpoon vessels are in sight now too. There are four of them on the horizon, which means that the *Yushin Marus 1, 2* and *3* and the *Shonan Maru No. 2* have all entered the fray.

After a short while, the *Nisshin Maru* gets going again. But since the ship now cruises at barely 5 knots, the prop fouler must have done something. At this speed, the *Bob Barker* should be able to catch up.

Our job is done. The captain of the *Bob Barker* informs us that they're going after the *Nisshin Maru*, but we tell them that we won't be coming along. There's no time to refuel us, which must now be done via the *Steve Irwin*. We are given food, however. The kitchen will pack provisions in an old survival suit and throw it overboard. A survival suit floats, so we'll just fish it out of the water.

Pete's frustrated at having to drop out. 'This is really shit. It's like being at a party with lots of good food and drink and plenty of women. And it gets better and better as the evening progresses, but just when it's really taking off you suddenly have to go and collect your mother at the airport.'

He allows the *Ady Gil* to drop back so the *Bob Barker* can catch up. For a while we sail parallel to our other ship, gently, at a couple of knots. Two harpoon vessels steam ahead and pull up dangerously close. But Jimmy and his spud gun remain inside; there's no need for provocation now. The *Ady Gil* doesn't alter its course, which is Pete's way of saying that we're not taking any more action. The harpoon vessels pick up speed as they make for the mother ship. Pete is full of admiration.

'They're such beautiful vessels. So well-built. Look at them slice through the water. Incredible.'

The *Bob Barker* approaches on starboard side. We position ourselves behind the ship. I wave at Amber, an old-timer who, along with a couple of unfamiliar crew members, slips a survival suit into the water. The *Ady Gil* swoops down on it and together we lug the stuffed survival suit onto the afterdeck. Those who are free lend a hand and carry the food to our little kitchen. Cartons of fruit juice, chocolate bars, tinned vegetables and freshly baked bread rolls. We're over the moon. Now we'll definitely hold out until the *Steve Irwin* reaches us.

'Fresh blueberry pancakes,' I tell the crew, drooling at the prospect. After our kidney bean diet, we're looking at a veritable feast.

We sail past the *Bob Barker* one last time to wish the crew good luck. Jason takes the helm from the captain, so he too can join us and wave goodbye. On deck, I recognise veterans from previous years. We all wave and cheer. Peter and Amber are on the bridge with Captain Swift by their side. 'Good luck,' we yell at the top of our lungs. 'Give them hell,' Pete shouts. The fleeting encounter is a huge boost. After weeks in isolation, this contact with the other Sea Shepherd volunteers shows that the campaign is still in full swing.

As soon as the *Bob Barker* has passed, Pete signals for Jason to let the engines idle, so we don't use more fuel than necessary. One of the harpoon vessels overtakes the *Bob Barker* on starboard side, while the security vessel we saw earlier, the *Shonan Maru No. 2*, approaches us from behind.

Our unsuspecting team is sitting on the roof of the bobbing *Ady Gil*. Only Jason is still inside, at the helm. Mike leans against one of the fin-shaped exhausts with a photo camera in his hand.

'Try to get a good shot of the LRAD,' I tell him. He leans further forward.

'We won't be intimidated,' Pete says as the *Shonan Maru* approaches on port side.

'Let's keep staring at them.' The harpoon vessel is coming closer and closer. The shrill beeping of the LRAD is gaining in strength. 'Ow, ow, that hurts,' the captain and I say while laughing and jerking our bodies around. We draw a laugh from the team. 'Somebody get me out of here. I can't hack it anymore,' I groan in jest. The LRAD gets louder.

'That's pretty painful actually,' Mike says, and he's right: the sound cannon has been cranked up to 'deafening'. The security vessel seems to be passing, but just when she has almost overtaken the *Ady Gil*, the *Shonan Maru* pulls to the right, her bow pushing into the swell.

First swell: the bow is headed straight for our ship.

Second swell: the harpoon vessel is on a collision course.

'Watch out,' Pete yells in a blind panic. I'm standing on top of the *Ady Gil* with the bow of a 700-tonne steel ship towering above me. There's no escape. There's no time to think. With a feline reflex I jump onto our stern and grab hold of two wooden boards fixed there. The Japanese vessel bores straight into the *Ady Gil*'s side. Our bow creaks and shatters. An enormous wave washes over us. I hang on for dear life so as not to be swept overboard.

The *Ady Gil* is rammed with such force that the boat nearly capsizes. As it lifts out of the water, the left float briefly hovers precariously over my head. Then it slams back onto the water. A powerful jet hits my body: a water cannon at the back of the *Shonan Maru* is giving us a thrashing. The security vessel spurts away, leaving the *Ady Gil* in its wake, cut in half. Disorientation follows.

I'm still alive. Am I still alive? Yes, I'm still alive. I can't think straight. There are long, elusive pauses between my thoughts. I want to flex and relax my muscles, but I can't move. Paralysed, I stare at the departing security vessel. Outside stimuli fail to reach my senses. I can't hear a thing. All I see is the *Shonan Maru No. 2* without fully realising what has just happened.

'Mayday, send a mayday call,' Pete yells in the direction of the cockpit. Our captain is still alive. As soon as I come to my senses I realise that we're not out of danger yet. Jimmy, Mike and Simeon are standing nearby on the afterdeck, visibly shaken but still alive. Jason's in the cockpit, white as a sheet but still breathing. Behind the chief engineer, seawater is gushing into the *Ady Gil*. The front has been completely knocked away and a gaping hole is spewing our things into the sea: backpack, sleeping bag, clothes, laptop, iPod, books – just about everything I own is being spat out by the *Ady Gil*. Everything that doesn't sink at once slowly drifts away.

Pete and Jimmy carry an inflatable life raft outside. Mike is busy launching the jet-ski, so we'll have more space on the stern, while the cameraman is trying to bring his tapes to safety on the afterdeck. The mayday has been picked up by the *Bob Barker*, which is doing a U-turn and launching the rubber boats. The skipper runs back inside.

'Grab the passports and the logbook,' I call after him. Everything that can be saved is laid out on the stern. The ship is taking on water – Jason is standing up to his ankles in the freezing water – but it's not going into the engine room.

'As long as the floats are intact and the engine room doesn't fill up, the ship will stay afloat,' Pete reckons. The New Zealander's assumption stops us from abandoning the ship in a panic.

Very gradually, the reality of the attack sinks in. 'They ran us down. Fuck man, they just ran us down,' the cameraman says in shock. Pete inspects the damage. The floats are damaged, but not broken. The tip of the *Ady Gil* floats a bit further away. It's a dismal sight.

'I'm glad I'm still alive, really glad,' Mike sighs. 'One or two more metres to the right and the ship would have run over us.' His eyes fill with tears as his thoughts drift to his young daughter, who was very nearly fatherless.

I clamber onto the roof of the *Ady Gil* and cut our flags from the antennas. Whatever happens, the Japanese won't get hold of our flags. The campaign flag and the Sea Shepherd flag are obviously not priorities, but since they symbolise our battle they mustn't fall into Japanese hands.

The rubber boats approach and carry us to the *Bob Barker*. Pottsy, my room-mate from Operation Musashi, is the first to hug me when I step on board the Sea Shepherd ship. I've no idea what he's saying, except that I fall into his arms and hug him tight. My voice falters, I've got tears in my eyes and my legs are trembling under me. More hugs follow. I'm so pleased to see everyone, and so pleased to be alive.

'Good to see you,' says Captain Swift. 'I just wish the circumstances were different.' I'm silent. What can I say? We just saw our ship, our home for the past few weeks, get shattered in seconds.

Amber throws herself around my neck. I give her a tight hug. A hug feels good when you've almost perished. Peter's next.

'Is everyone all right?' the first mate asks.

'Yes, I think so. Simeon's hurt his ribs, but it's nothing serious.'

'You guys have been incredibly lucky. You'd better call your parents, by the way, because these images are about to go global.'

Of course, this will make the news around the world. The cameras on board the *Bob Barker* have captured every moment of the collision and the media team is busy preparing a news item. This is the ultimate in sensationalist TV.

I should call my mum and dad. Peter hands me a satellite phone. From Antarctica I contact De Lier, where my parents are fast asleep.

'Theo speaking.'

'Dad, it's Lau. I've been rammed. I mean, our ship's been rammed. We're sinking. That's to say our ship's sinking, not me. We're fine. We were rescued by our other ship.' I'm so emotional the words just spill out of my mouth. I want to tell him everything in just a couple of seconds.

'Huh, what?' I tell him the story again, more slowly this time. I reckon it's still not sinking in, because his next question is: 'Right, do you want to speak to your mother?'

A bit taken aback, I stare at the satellite phone. 'Uh… no, that's OK. The others have to call too. Speak to you soon, bye.'

'OK, take care, bye.'

No sympathetic noises or calming words. It was only when they saw the dreadful images on the news that my parents realised what had happened. It just goes to prove Captain Watson's words: 'If we haven't recorded it, it effectively never happened.'

The *Bob Barker* is forced to halt its pursuit of the *Nisshin Maru*. The crew spends the rest of the day salvaging our ship. Just about everything that could sink has indeed sunk, but luckily they managed to fish my backpack and sleeping bag out of the water. Some of the belongings of the others were recovered as well. Once the peace aboard the ship has been restored, we're told to have a shower, since our stench is unbearable. I have to borrow clean underwear.

At the back of the *Bob Barker* a room is cleared where the six of us get to sleep. It's cramped, but we're used to that by now.

That evening, quite exceptionally, we're served a drink. The *Ady Gil* crew is seated at a table in the mess. In our borrowed clothes and with our freshly washed faces we finally look more or less presentable again. We gaze intently into each other's eyes. We clink glasses and propose a toast.

To the *Ady Gil*.

To our team.

To escaping death.

To luck.

To life.

We fall asleep drunk. In my dreams, a killed motorcyclist finally leaves me alone.

31

HOME SWEET HOME

A sad fate awaits the *Ady Gil*. It looks wretched trailing behind the *Bob Barker*. The towing rope has already snapped once and the shell is taking on more and more water. Towing is pointless since the mainland is too far. Besides, Sea Shepherd is losing far too much ground to the whalers. The futuristic trimaran is a lost cause.

Her proud erstwhile captain wants to execute the sentence himself. Pete waits until most of the crew are asleep and then, in the middle of the night, he fouls the *Ady Gil* so it will sink faster and won't be a danger to other vessels.

The following morning I see that the *Ady Gil* has disappeared. Somewhere behind us, the most beautiful boat in the world is sinking to the bottom of the ocean. The curtain has come down on our expedition.

Without our ship, we wander aimlessly around the *Bob Barker*. Most of us want to get back to the mainland as quickly as possible. Mike more than anyone, because his job is on the line. He's having argument after raging argument with the captain, who first promises to take Mike to Antarctica or Australia before changing his mind and saying it can't be done. It's driving the firefighter mad and he refuses to make himself useful on board. He withdraws to our room and rarely comes out. Jason and Jimmy help out where they can, while I lend a hand in the kitchen and do occasional shifts as quartermaster. Pete vows revenge.

The *Bob Barker* receives orders taking it to the Kerguelen Islands. The *Steve Irwin* is moored in the French territory while the harpoon vessel that was chasing her waits outside the territorial waters. When we hook up with our flagship, the Gilbillies transfer. The *Steve Irwin* has problems with its helicopter and will have to have some parts replaced in Fremantle in Australia. The *Bob Barker* stays behind. During a storm she manages to elude her Japanese pursuers and continues her hunt for the *Nisshin Maru*.

En route to Fremantle Captain Watson offers me a choice: stay on board or travel to Europe to manage Sea Shepherd's European operations. After three years of volunteering, the prospect of a paid position is more tempting than adventure, and besides, to me this campaign is finished. The ship that was my home has split in two and sunk. This is the end of Operation Waltzing Matilda as far as I'm concerned. And Europe, that means back to my family and my long-awaited first date with Andrea.

With the exception of Pete, the whole team leaves the *Steve Irwin* in Fremantle. In the past few months I've shared the good and the bad with these men, but our farewell is an odd one. Jason and Mike are off before the crack of dawn. Only Jimmy stays in town for a couple of days. I wish the skipper and Sea Shepherd crew good luck and with that my campaign is over.

Pete returns to Antarctica, determined to have his revenge. On 15 February 2010 the New Zealand daredevil jumps on board the *Shonan Maru No. 2* and confronts the captain with his actions. It doesn't come to blows, but the stowaway is arrested and transported to Japan. At long last, the captain of the *Ady Gil* gets his fifteen minutes of fame by making the news all over the world, even though it comes with a three-month prison sentence and a costly court case.

Whoever is to blame for the attack is still a moot point. To us it's crystal clear: we were rammed. But the captain of the *Shonan Maru* has never been questioned, let alone convicted. The maritime authorities in New Zealand, where the *Ady Gil* was registered, carried out an investigation. But despite the fact that the collision was the best-documented attack ever, they concluded that there was insufficient evidence to identify a guilty party. Both captains were negligent and that was that.

Pete Bethune and Sea Shepherd didn't part on friendly terms.* A financial dispute earned our adventure on the *Ady Gil* a black mark in the chronicles of Sea Shepherd's Antarctica campaigns. But not for me. Never. Not that long ago, I travelled in a small ferry from the Indonesian island of Gili Air to the mainland of Bali. I was at the rear, squeezed in among sweaty tourists, inhaling diesel fumes with the noise of throbbing engines in the background. But when I closed my eyes I was back in the fresh breeze on the roof of the incomparable *Ady Gil*, together with five brave men who were determined to protect the whales of the South Pole. We were accompanied by three humpbacks singing a timeless ballad. The song caressed my ears until the ferry moored in Padang Bai. Thankfully you have some control over your memories.

During Operation Waltzing Matilda the Sea Shepherd crew managed to disrupt the illegal Japanese whale hunt for quite some time. Despite the loss of the *Ady Gil*, the campaign resulted in 528 saved whales.

In response to this campaign, Australia decided to bring a case against Japan for illegal whaling around Antarctica. The case is currently before the International Court of Justice. A ruling is expected in early 2014.

---

* Pete Bethune continues to do conservation work with his own organisation: Earthrace Conservation – www.earthraceconservation.org

THE FORGOTTEN
HUNT

32

THIS IS AFRICA

At dusk, chilly banks of fog turn the Namib Desert into an eerie wilderness, all but obscuring the ragged rock formations and the vast sandy beach. By the time the world is completely swallowed up, all visitors have long since returned to the warm hotels of Swakopmund. Nobody wants to stay here if they don't have to. Legend has it that at night this country is given over to the wandering ghosts of dead mariners who dwell in the rotting shipwrecks just off the coast. 'Let's get the hell out of here' was the motto of the intrepid explorers who named the area Cape Cross. 'Welcome!' it now says at the entrance to the nature reserve. But only between 10 and 5. Outside opening hours it's 'no trespassing', so the Cape fur seals, which have been living here for hundreds of years, can get some peace and quiet. That's what the tourists are told anyway.

The reality is that the shady slaughtering practices of the cruel seal hunters must be hidden from outsiders. If people knew what was happening to these gorgeous animals, Namibia's second largest tourist attraction wouldn't get any visitors. It would fail to attract foreign dollars and the hunters would be forced to halt their practices. And that's exactly what we're trying to achieve.

'Thanks for making a little time for us,' Steve Roest is told when, two days later than planned, he strolls into our safe house. Our team leader is not amused. He dumps his suitcases in a corner of the living room and slumps into a chair, exhausted.

'What a mess. When I got to Johannesburg, I wasn't allowed to travel on to Namibia because they claimed my passport was too full. Next up, the embassy was closed. When I got into a cab the following day, it drove to the wrong side of town. When I finally made it to the embassy, they were just closing and told me to come back in a couple of hours. And you know what the guy behind the counter told me after hours of frustration? "TIA, sir. This Is Africa. In Africa nothing ever goes to plan." All right, TIA, but I'm here now. What are we doing?'

Training is the response. The fog provides a perfect cover for us to leave the road unseen and test our equipment. We're off in about 30 minutes. Most of us are ready, dressed in bulletproof vests and with night-vision goggles tied around our foreheads. Our latest team member gets no time to recover. Shortly after midnight, we exit the gate of our back garden in Swakopmund. Nikki Botha holds the fort. The South African says she's not afraid of anyone. She's perfectly capable of guarding our house at 24 Sapphire Street on her own, so we can all go out and train.

Ahead of us, the curtain of fog gets thicker and thicker as we leave the coastal town behind. The unlit road is deserted, shrouded in darkness. The headlights of my off-road vehicle have difficulty penetrating the low-hanging cloud. The haze reduces our visibility to just a couple of metres. Doing no more than 30 kilometres per hour our convoy drives along the only salt road towards Henties Bay.

'Lights out,' Ralph whispers over the walkie-talkie. We navigate the next several hundred metres through the blanket of clouds without lights before taking a right turn and going off-road. Somewhere on the salt plain, far from the main road, we come to a standstill. This is an excellent spot: nobody will find us here. We listen quietly for any pursuers. Not a soul. We get started. The lights remain off: we'll have to do our exercise in pitch-darkness.

The team has to figure out how fast it can place cameras without being detected. Our aim is to film the seal hunt and broadcast the images in a television documentary. Watched by millions, the senseless hunt will finally get the negative attention it deserves. Hopefully, worldwide pressure on the Namibian government will then force even the most corrupt officials to put a stop to the massacre.

Julie Andersen and Dinielle Stöckigt handle the cameras. The rest of us practise with our night-vision goggles and GPS. As soon as we're all used to the lack of depth perception and we've stopped stumbling, we carry a transmitter on an improvised stretcher across the plain. The device weighs a ton, but is essential, because we're planning to bury the cameras and operate them via remote control. The transmitter allows the signal to be transmitted across 10 kilometres: more than enough to keep clear of the security around Cape Cross. It all sounds like child's play, but implementing the plan has been a nightmare from day one. 'Extremely user-friendly' our team member Rupert was promised by the specialist company that sold him the cameras. They conveniently forgot to mention that you need a crane to move the transmitter. It takes four guys to haul the bloody thing across the sand.

'Stick together, don't shout and absolutely no lights,' I stress once more. I have to be this strict because I know what has happened in the past to activists who were caught filming the Namibian seal slaughter: they were beaten up, had their equipment stolen and were put in prison by corrupt police officers. And that was just 'a caution'. When the seal clubbers find out that Sea Shepherd is active here it probably won't stop at a warning. A human life matters little in this dirt-poor country, and besides, it's easy to disappear in the vast wilderness of the Skeleton Coast, where ominous waves batter the shore and a huge desert puts paid to any chances of survival.

Ralph, Steve, Rupert and I carry the transmitter, Dinielle and Julie follow the men, while Rosie and Grace keep watch by the cars. Without a sound, we walk several hundred metres into the darkness. 'Here's good,' says Steve. 'Let's test the signal.'

While the cameras synchronise with the transmitter, we suddenly hear Rosie over the walkie-talkie. 'Come in, guys, come in.'

Were we followed, after all? Steve replies: 'What's up, Rosie?'

'Nikki just called, our house is being broken into.'

'What? We're on our way!'

During the short-lived panic that follows we all think of our mate alone in the house.

'Come, back to the cars,' Ralph shouts, leading the way with a camera under his arm. The usually so unflappable kung fu instructor is in a real state and wants to get back to our house as quickly as possible. The rest of us gather up the equipment and run back to the Land Cruisers as fast as the fog allows. We chuck everything in the boot and drive back to the town centre. There's so much low-hanging cloud the salt road seems to merge with the plain. Only the occasional marker post by the side of the road tells us where to go. We can't do more than 40 kilometres per hour; it takes us ages.

Nikki is waiting for us with a neighbour. The four-wheel drive hasn't even come to a complete standstill when Rupert jumps out and storms into the house. It's pointless of course. The burglars have long since fled with our valuables, leaving only a broken window and bits of glass on the floor, like silent witnesses.

With tears trickling down her cheeks Nikki mumbles that she's let the team down.

'Nonsense,' I reassure her, and put my arm around her. We're so relieved that she's OK. This is, after all, Southern Africa – serious violent crime, including rape, is common here.

'God damn it,' Rupert yells, while whipping cushions off the sofa in the hope of retrieving some of his stolen property. 'My passport, they've nicked my passport, damn it!' It's not only his most important travel document that's missing; video and photo cameras, mobile phones, money, credit cards and laptops are gone too. Here we are, on day one of our campaign, and Operation Desert Seal is already heading for disaster.

According to Nikki, there were three burglars. The black men forced their way into the house from the back. She tried to chase them away by screaming, but they carried on regardless. Eventually she climbed through the bedroom window and fled to the next-door neighbours.

The neighbour explains that the perpetrators are probably from Mondesa, a slum area within walking distance. He says it's not the first time that this corner house has been targeted. I look at Steve: that would explain why Rupert was able to rent this villa at such a knock-down price.

While we're inside, making an inventory of the missing items, the local police arrive on the scene. The driver is dressed in a light grey suit, which could, with the necessary imagination, be construed as a uniform. His co-driver is wearing a camouflage outfit. He yawns repeatedly before he gets out of the car. Judging by his blood-shot eyes, the officer has only just woken up.

Both policemen give the house the once-over and then announce they're off to find the perpetrators. Weird. The break-in happened more than 30 minutes ago. Besides, there's no sign of any footprints and the streets are filled with thick fog. And yet these seasoned sleuths reckon they can catch the crooks. Without another word, the police speed off.

Within less than half an hour the dedicated detectives are back.

'We found them,' the camouflaged officer says with fake delight. 'But you see, they ran away when they saw us.'

He pauses briefly before he launches into his exciting denouement. 'But we did retrieve some things.' He hands us a rucksack with broken camera lenses, two photo cameras, empty wallets and other missing items. The laptops are still gone, as is Rupert's passport.

'Wow, incredible that you guys found those crooks.' The officers flash a macho grin.

I don't believe an effing word of their story: in this nocturnal mist it's impossible to find anyone, least of all burglars who are swallowed up by a labyrinthine township. I can't prove it, but I bet these police officers are working hand in glove with the criminals. They're only returning some of our things because they expect us 'westerners' to pay a finder's fee. They hang around longer than necessary. These officers won't get a penny: I'm not keen on criminals, but I absolutely loathe corrupt police.

We end the impasse by asking 'what do we do now?'

The coppers look at one another.

'Um, you guys have to go to the station to report the crime. We'll be on our way now.' There's no such thing as fingerprinting or forensics around here. Foregoing their tip, the officers get back into their patrol car. Without a left rear light, but with peeling paint and rust on the doors, it vanishes in the mist.

When all is calm again, we draw up the balance: thousands of dollars' worth of cash, cameras, mobile phones, laptops, credit cards and Rupert's passport are gone. And what's more: our safe house has been compromised. Tomorrow we're off to a new location, which we have yet to find. The weird thing is that the memory cards in the retrieved cameras are missing. Hopefully the burglars chucked them away in their hurry, because if anyone sees our photos we can expect some tough questions. This close to Cape Cross and the opening of the hunting season, the authorities can only draw one conclusion: those guys are here for the seals.

Steve and I are outside on the veranda, catching our breath after the stressful experience.

'Pretty shit,' I sum up the day.

Steve pushes a finger down the neck of his beer bottle to pull the air out. With a big gulp he washes away today's unpleasant aftertaste.

'First my passport, now this, what a start. And those corrupt officers. There's something fishy going on.'

'They're watching us.'

'Who are?'

'Those guys in the townships, or those officers, or… fuck, who knows. We're threatening the livelihood of the seal hunters. I bet everybody here is against us.'

'We're the underdogs. All the more reason not to give up. But it sucks that we have to improvise this early on.'

'Hang on, it's the first time we're doing this campaign in Africa. And let's be honest, a couple of months ago in the pub we didn't expect everything to go to plan. Besides…' A grin steals over my face. 'This Is Africa.'

'You can say that again,' Steve sighs with the hint of a smile, 'T… I… A… This Is Africa.'

33

OPERATION DESERT SEAL

A few months earlier , in the White Cross Pub, Richmond, England.

So far the cheery Australian has been talking non-stop about his campaign against the dolphin hunt in Taiji in Japan. That Rupert Imhoff is passionate about marine life is patently obvious after only five minutes.

Having had a taste of campaigning, he's now trying to channel his unbridled enthusiasm into convincing Sea Shepherd CEO Steve Roest of the need for a new campaign.

'Every year more than 85,000 baby seals are clubbed to death for their fur in Namibia. Very few people are aware of this. Everybody knows about the Canadian hunt, with those little white seals, whereas the number of seals killed is actually far lower. The Namibian government is keeping this African cull carefully concealed from the outside world. Why? Because the vast majority are clubbed to death in a tourist area that generates an annual revenue of millions of dollars. And those animals are only slaughtered because the Fisheries Ministry claims they're eating all the fish. They're supposedly protecting the fishermen.'

Untrue and unfounded. It's the Namibian fishermen who are extirpating the fish, not the seals who have been living off the African coast for hundreds, if not thousands of years. Did you know that Robben Island, where Nelson Mandela was imprisoned, was once known for its seals? They're all gone now, because the South Africans killed every last one of them. The hunt has since been banned over there, but if Namibia keeps at it there won't be any seals left. They really ought to manage their fishing industry. Nearly 300 fishing vessels scour the coast and plunder their own waters. And that's not counting all the foreign vessels that poach the African seas.

It's a question of trade, pure and simple, according to Rupert, who has clearly read up on the matter. He explains that the government receives a fixed sum for each clubbed seal. The Turkish-Australian fur trader Hatem Yavuz buys up all the velvety baby skins, turns them into the latest fur fashions and sells them at huge profits in Asia and elsewhere. But the other parts bring in money too. In China the seal penises are sold as aphrodisiacs.

Along with the licensees and a bunch of corrupt officials, Yavuz makes a very good living off the seal slaughter. And to think that the tourist industry actually earns millions of euros more from living seals than the hunters do from dead ones.

The example Rupert cites is the Cape Cross colony in the West Coast National Park. All tourists pay at least $10 per visit. The park draws more than a hundred thousand tourists annually. As well as a great deal of money, it creates dozens of jobs throughout the year. But instead of cherishing this beautiful place, Namibia allows some 15 hunters a day to come in between 1 July and 15 November to slaughter the young seals for a couple of dollars per hour.

'The cull makes no sense at all, neither ecologically nor economically,' concludes a very grave-looking Rupert.

My head is spinning with all this information. So is Steve's. Since my experiences on the *Ady Gil* some months ago, I've been working as Director of European Operations for Sea Shepherd, executing campaigns from my base in Europe. And now, sitting in a quiet west London pub and listening to this untold horror story, it's clear that something needs to be done. Gradually, ideas start to take shape. But before we develop them any further, I have a question: 'How come hardly anyone knows about this?'

'No idea. The hunt has been filmed before, but the images never reached a wide audience. Now the whole thing is dated and nobody's interested. Besides, the Namibian government is keeping the cull a secret, since the hunters are clubbing the seals in a national sanctuary – hardly the best possible PR.'

'Is it illegal?' Steve needs to know in order to justify a Sea Shepherd action.

'Yes. And no,' Rupert equivocates. 'Namibia says it's legal. The Fisheries Ministry issues licences and claims that the fur seals are a threat to fish stocks.'

So far, so clear. Beyond that, the whole thing gets murky. The government has never produced any scientific evidence to prove that the seals are eating the fish.

'Something they share with Japan, which has never published a single study into their harpooned whales,' I think out loud.

'Exactly. It's just as dodgy. And to top it all, the government dismisses every challenge as manipulated data from animal activists. It won't sanction independent monitoring of the hunt, or indeed any filming or photography, which is in conflict with the freedom of the press guaranteed by the constitution.

'No prizes for guessing why Namibia won't allow the hunt to be filmed. Bashing in baby seal skulls looks anything but "humane". But that's exactly how the government describes the hunt. Namibia's animal protection law ought to apply to these seals, but the politicians believe that, according to the letter of the law, the Cape fur seals aren't "animals".'

Steve raises his eyebrows.

'The law states that "wild animals" aren't animals as covered by the law.'

'Finally,' Rupert concludes, 'the Cape fur seals fall under list II of the CITES treaty that regulates trade in endangered species. That means that the species isn't under threat provided the necessary controls on both hunt and trade are in place. Well, there are no such controls.'

Steve and I know enough. There are plenty of sentimental reasons for stopping this barbaric practice, but now we have the legal arguments to back them up. That said, the time to prepare for an operation in Africa is tight. April is nearly over, we have no budget for this campaign, the Sea Shepherd board has yet to give us permission and we need reconnaissance on the ground. The latter is sorted with a nod to Rupert. He promises to book a flight to the capital Windhoek as soon as possible and at his own expense.

That leaves the question: how are we going to tackle the hunt? Via land and sea, so we can spread the risks and increase our chances of capturing images of the cull. For the sea journey we'll need a small vessel. In the event we can't film directly from the boat, we can consider going ashore in a rubber boat and hiding out in the dunes.

A land mission is more straightforward. From the hinterland the seal colony is relatively easy to get to. The hills around Cape Cross provide sufficient cover, Rupert reckons, having already looked at Google Earth. That's the campaign drafted. Now all we need is for Steve to get permission from Captain Paul Watson.

Before we say goodbye, we put together a possible team. I only have one request: Ralph Herde, my former Wing Chun instructor from Melbourne. His martial arts skills are unrivalled and he knows everything there is to know about four-wheel drives. I have a sneaking suspicion that both skills could come in handy.

A couple of days later Steve sends word that we've been given the go-ahead. The campaign plan has been dubbed Operation Desert Seal. The Sea Shepherd director will remain in the US for now to secure a production team for a TV documentary. I start raising funds.

By mid-May our fundraising efforts are finally paying off. After umpteen refusals, it looks like two wealthy backers may be prepared to finance the campaign. A dinner with Paul Watson in Cannes should win them over.

The boat we've been invited to is anchored off the rocks of Île Saint-Marguerite, where a fabulous view of the old prison, Fort Royal, inspires Paul to tell anecdotes about famous pirates. A bottle of wine is opened. The delicious bouquet of expensive red wine is a mark of the host's admiration for Captain Watson's unique marine conservation work.

While we're on our main course, the reason for the meeting is broached. You get one chance to make a pitch, especially with business people who are begged all year round to donate their fortune to good causes.

The seals, the cruelty, the illegality, our plan: all in just a couple of minutes. Less is more. The idea receives a positive response. Neither donor has the slightest reservation, so later that same evening we return to the mainland with the cheques in our pockets.

The news from Namibia is good too. Cape Cross can be filmed from the sea, Rupert writes in his report. The rough breakers make landing on the beach in a rubber boat difficult, but not impossible. Having studied Cape Cross and its surroundings, he reckons he knows exactly what we need and he takes care of much of the logistics.

Towards the end of June the team arrives in Cape Town. Our small, second-hand ship should arrive in the South African coastal city in a couple of days' time. And at the eleventh hour, Steve has managed to secure a professional camera team to produce an episode of *Seal Wars* in collaboration with Animal Planet. Only Paul Watson is still missing. Bringing the Sea Shepherd figurehead into Namibia is a huge risk, but Steve and I are determined to have him. Nobody can plead quite so passionately for an end to the culling. Paul is travelling under his own steam in an effort to remain under the radar. We want to avoid a 'preventative' deportation.

Now that we're almost complete, we embark on the long journey northwards. Bulletproof vests and night-vision goggles have been hidden behind the side compartments of our four-wheel drives. We're nervous as we cross the border at Vioolsdrif.

The border guards are half asleep at the counter and stamp our passports without a single question. They don't even ask where our journey is taking us. Which is just as well, because we'd like to remain anonymous for now.

34

THE FACTORY FROM HELL

The salt road from Swakopmund to Cape Cross is largely deserted. We drive 120 kilometres across the arid plain, where the odd shipwreck protrudes above the sand dunes. Every now and then we're overtaken by an open pick-up truck carrying Africans in threadbare, dirty clothes. Deep furrows in their sombre faces reflect the hard life in the Namibian mines. The poor around here don't have a lot of choice. In much of the country unemployment is over 50 per cent. Those who manage to find a job will do everything in their power to keep it. The same applies to the seal hunters of Henties Bay.

For less than $6 a day, the uneducated men of this small coastal village are prepared to do whatever their white employer tells them to. And while these poor Namibians are condemned to a life under corrugated sheets that offer little protection from the blistering sun and the sea wind, the licensee fills his pockets at their expense. He shares his earnings with Yavuz, who's making a killing from the fur trade. Complain and you're out. You wouldn't know any of this reading the glossy brochures luring anglers from all over the world to this African fishing village.

The salt road winds its way through the Namib Desert. We have the Atlantic Ocean with its fertile fishing grounds on the driver's side, while the black rocks of the Lagunen Hills loom on the right. Lining the road are stalls made out of driftwood with pink salt crystals sweating beside crooked cardboard signs. The stalls, like the landscape, are deserted. The stallholders are said to live in the abandoned salt mines around Cape Cross, but there are no signs of life. Only an empty glass jar inviting customers to pay a handful of Namibian dollars.

If you keep following the road along the Skeleton Coast you end up in neighbouring Angola. We turn left towards the seal colony of Cape Cross.

After the burglary our team could do with a boost and what better medicine than seeing our clients, the Cape fur seals? The entrance gates are wide open and a sign indicates the opening hours: 8 a.m.–5 p.m. Strange, we thought the hunt carried on until 10 in the morning. The first thing we'll need to do is figure out what time the cull is actually taking place.

Further up, a few hundred metres from the entrance, in one of the bays, is the Cape Cross Lodge, where visitors can relish the glorious emptiness around them. They're unaware of the bloodbath at dawn. The hills between the Lodge and the seal colony screen the hunt and the howling wind drowns out the dying seals' screams.

The stench of dead fish hangs over the tens of thousands of Cape fur seals resting on the beach of Cape Cross. A couple of bulls start baying when we set foot on the platform for the tourists. Otherwise, the seals largely ignore us. Pups are gathered in nurseries which are watched over by the females. Their little eyes open briefly when we walk past, and immediately close again when they realise we pose no threat. Likewise, the sluggish mothers stay put on the sand. Relaxed, they raise their heads a little, sniff the air and fall asleep again.

Out in the water, a group of seals is playing in the breakers. Lanky bodies dive into the waves and disappear under water for several minutes before reappearing on the beach with fish. Along with the odd jackal, the bulls in this gorgeous nature reserve are the only threat to the baby seals. Occasionally, the hefty males will charge at the young ones. But the pups are quick learners. With their front flippers they shuffle back to mama in the nursery where they're safe.

I wonder what this place will be like in a couple of weeks' time, when the clubbers set to work on their barbaric task every morning.

As we walk along the wooden deck, we're all plunged into our own sad thoughts. Julie and Grace are crying, because they know we can't put an immediate stop to the terrible cull. Veterinary surgeon André makes notes in a small notebook, trying to take in as many details as possible.

With the animals playing in the background, Paul Watson, who arrived the day before, explains why this annual baby seal cull must be stopped. This 'Seal War', waged on behalf of the Namibian seals, is going to take a lot of time and patience, the Sea Shepherd captain predicts. The hunt for the white seals in Canada has been effectively shut down, but it took decades to achieve this. It may be the same over here.

As soon as the producer is happy with Paul's sound bites, we leave again. We'd rather remain unnoticed. Sea Shepherd may be in a remote area of Africa, but even in these parts the locals can receive Animal Planet. Paul had the impression that a petrol station attendant in Windhoek recognised him. There's clearly a flipside to the popularity of *Whale Wars*.

The Sea Shepherd founder spends one more day in Swakopmund to go over the plans with us and to visit the slaughterhouse. He wants to see it with his own eyes.

Luckily dusk falls early in Namibia, so we can observe the large factory building just outside Henties Bay in the dark without drawing attention to ourselves. There appears to be no security. Having made sure of this, we drive onto the site with our lights off. Our surroundings turn pale green when we don our night-vision goggles. Steve and I walk around the premises to double-check if anyone's there.

Round the back we recognise the green pickup mentioned in Rupert's briefing documents. It's used for transporting the dead seals. The nets are wet, but there's no trace of the animals. Nothing suggests that the hunting season is underway, even though the processing plant looks ready. We peer through the windows: the room is filled with large chains with hooks for the cadavers, grinders for the meat, huge pots, knives with razor-sharp blades to cut the pelts off the flesh and other medieval bits of machinery that I can't immediately place. The thought of the protected seals getting chopped up sends shivers down my spine. Looking at this plant, I can only think one thing: raze it to the ground. Ideally, I'd bulldoze it tonight.

Steve signals for us to leave. As soon as we turn onto the road, a pair of bright headlights flash on behind us. The car must be on the factory site. Where it's come from all of a sudden is a mystery to us. So as not to arouse any suspicion, I calmly turn onto the C34 towards Swakopmund. The car races after us and stays on my tail. I can see the full beam headlights in my rear-view mirror. Something's not quite right. But there's no time to think. I step on the gas and tear along the salt road. I can't stay here; there's no way I can shake him off on this long, straight road. No sooner do I realise this than I take a sharp turn and enter Henties Bay.

Our car zips into a residential neighbourhood. Our pursuer follows suit. Left, right, right, left, two hands on the wheel, hand-over-hand, lights off and braking with the hand brake: the instructions from my police driving lessons come flooding back. Steve and Paul peer through the rear window to see if the car is still following us. It is. I put my foot down. A few more corners, then I come to a standstill. I park the car in a front yard, roll the windows up and stop the engine.

We all duck. We can hear an engine throbbing nearby. Now far, then closer again. Quiet as a mouse, we listen to the car that's looking for us. Our trick seems to be working: the noise disappears, leaving only the stillness of the African night.

When we're absolutely certain that our pursuer is gone, I weave my way back to the road to Swakopmund. Miraculously, nobody is waiting for us. We drive back to our safe house as fast as we can.

Although the pursuit had a happy ending, it's highly likely that word about our visit to the factory will get around. In no time the whole region will know that something is afoot. With our white faces we're simply asking for trouble.

We have to get a move on: early tomorrow morning Ralph, Dinielle, Rosie, cameraman Mo, his bodyguard Kobe and I will travel to the desert behind Cape Cross. We'll take an indirect route. This 'desert team' will have to map out the slaughtering process as quickly as possible. The others travel back to the ship to strike from the water.

35

WARSHIPS OFF THE COAST

Having negotiated the long paved road to Otjiwarongo, the arid savannas around Khorixas and the almost impassable off-road stretches past the Brandberg Mountain, our Land Cruisers finally reach the rocky hills behind Cape Cross. There are no prying eyes here and the inhospitable region offers sufficient shelter for us to carry out our mission unseen. Across the hills is the road connecting the colony and Henties Bay, behind us the Namib Desert where the occasional herd of springboks bound across the barren plain. In this no-man's-land, we pitch our rooftop tents.

Tonight we're hoping to discover what time the cull actually kicks off. Around dawn, we suspect, but as long as we're not certain, we can't plan anything. Ralph and I set out to explore the area. The sun's beating down on us and our feet slip on the bits of broken rock covering the hills. After a 15-minute hike from the camp we come upon a rock formation overlooking the access road. Ralph finds a rock in which the salty sea wind has carved out a dark hole. A few metres away, between two rocks, I find a suitable spot for my camera. My GPS saves the waypoints and then we walk back to the camp for a catnap while the sun renders the desert unbearable.

To make sure we don't miss the death squad Ralph, Rosie and I are hiding out among the rocks around three o'clock the following morning. My camera is concealed in a small green bush that somehow manages to survive in this parched environment. All is quiet; the road remains empty for hours.

'Hey Lau,' whispers Rosie, lying a couple of metres behind me.

'Yeah?'

'Watch out for the snakes.'

'What do you mean?'

'This is prime territory for horned adders.'

It hadn't occurred to me.

'You love snakes, don't you?' Ralph joins her.

I can hear Rosie giggling in the background. They both know I loathe snakes. The lethal ones anyway, the ones whose venom kills in minutes. The South African and the Australian are comfortable with dangerous reptiles, whereas the mere thought of an adder slithering across the sand is enough to make me shiver.

'Bitch!' Rosie's in stitches.

From then on, I find it impossible to relax. Peering through my night-vision goggles I check every dip in the sand. Any rustling I hear, I jump up, shake the sand off my camouflage trousers and pace about. I can't wait for the sun to rise.

Finally, just after six, deliverance comes in the form of an orange glow creeping over the mountain ridges in the distance. Gradually, the traffic gets going again. To begin with it's mostly pick-up trucks with fishing rods in the back, tourists or local fishermen, not seal clubbers.

Only when the final stars have disappeared does a convoy emerge from the direction of Henties Bay. Out front is an off-road vehicle with red stripes – police or security. It's followed by a green lorry and by pick-ups with seal hunters in the back. Another security car closes the procession. We calculate that the hunters will reach the seal colony at 6.30 sharp. That gives them an hour and a half before the nature reserve opens its doors.

We can't see what's going on, but it's not hard to imagine what happens during 90 minutes of clubbing: the adult seals will take refuge in the sea, leaving the powerless pups all alone on the beach. They'll be trapped in the loose sand. One of the hunters will herd the babies together after which the others will beat them until their arms are sore and the seals have stopped moving. A sticker checks every single fur seal and stabs a sharp knife straight through the heart. And with the mother's milk still dripping from the mouths of the lifeless pups, the beach absorbs the blood from their wounds.

The cadavers are thrown onto the lorry and then, just before eight, the seal clubbers clear the area. The parents are left behind in the water, distressed but safe, while the first few tourists arrive at the entrance for a visit to the nature reserve.

The lorry transports dozens if not hundreds of baby seals to the factory in Henties Bay. Ralph and I film the procession with our cameras. As the pick-ups pass by, we see the ashen-faced hunters in the back, clubs clutched between their knees. A morning of spreading death and destruction is over. We're done with our filming for now: a small victory, as we finally know what time the hunt starts and finishes.

As soon as the convoy has disappeared from view, Ralph jumps out of his hole.

'I was scared shitless. Look.' He points to a corner of his dark hole. 'That creature was beside me all night.' A lethal black scorpion scurries behind some rocks, more scared of Ralph than the other way round. It makes me think of the horned adder again. On our way back to base camp I tell the others I'm a little nostalgic for Antarctica, where the only scary creatures were the blood-thirsty Japanese whalers. 'Pussy' is the unanimous verdict.

Dinielle is waiting for us with breakfast. The smell attracts a black-backed jackal, which circles our camp, but remains at a timid distance. Over food and a cup of coffee, we update Dinielle on our minor triumph. Now we can start planning our next move.

We go through a number of different scenarios, and towards the end of the afternoon, when the sun has begun its downward journey, Ralph and I set off to find a route to the seal colony. On top of one of the tallest hills, Ralph scans the area around the reservation. He talks while I take notes: 'To the right, the Cape Cross Lodge, to the left the colony, but the hills block our view. To its left, the salt plains and salt rivers. To the right... hang on...'

He holds his head still and points to a dot on the water.

'Take a look, that's... that's not a fishing vessel, is it?' The sea is calm, resplendent in the evening sun, and even with the naked eye I can see a grey ship off the coast.

'Surely not...' I snatch the binoculars out of Ralph's hands.

'What do you reckon? Navy?'

'Shit, shit, shit.'

'What do you see?'

'White markings, it's a patrol boat.'

Beyond the hills at Cape Cross, a second ship has now joined the first one.

'Jesus, another one, and it's bigger.'

'Two navy ships? That can't be a coincidence.'

'No, definitely not.'

I know from Rupert's briefing that Namibia has only three warships. Right now, two of them are in the bay of Cape Cross, just when the seal culling season has kicked off. Have the bribes reached the highest echelons of government?

'Are they on the look-out for us?'

'No idea. Maybe they received a tip-off. Damn, there's no point in our ship coming over now. They'll board it straightaway.'

'Or blast it out of the water.'

We hurry back to the camp, where I report to Steve via the satellite phone. To keep our spirits up, I suggest it might be an exercise. Perhaps the vessels will be gone tomorrow or the day after. 'Who knows,' Steve says, but I can tell from his voice that he's just as doubtful as I am.

Our ship will remain in Cape Town until further notice. It's a huge blow for the sea team, who were about to set off. Now we'll have to film via land. Not only is it a risky undertaking, but we also have to get a move on, because the longer we spend behind these hills the greater our chance of detection. We spend the rest of the day outlining a strategy: tomorrow night is the night.

36

ESCAPE THROUGH THE DESERT

I fix each team member with a penetrating stare. Those with doubts must speak up now. Nobody has any questions: the mission is clear. There's only one way to reach the colony and that's via the beach. With the navy vessels off the coast, a landing from the water is out of the question. The hotel is to the north, but the access road is guarded by armed security staff. Only a narrow strip of beach offers access to the seals.

The route is lined by some dilapidated buildings dating back to the time when this area boasted a thriving mining industry. A few along the road are still occupied, but the hovels along the coast are uninhabitable. They constitute no risk. That's to say, we didn't see anyone during our reconnaissance.

We'll start when the tide is out, so the sea will wipe away our footprints over the course of the night. The initial plan to install remote-controlled cameras has been abandoned; the equipment is too heavy and bulky. We're going to film the massacre manually.

By dawn, we ought to have dug ourselves into the beach grass-covered dunes around the seal colony. As soon as the cull is over, Rosie and Dinielle will pick us up again at Cape Cross.

Team members Mo, Kobe and Ralph are eating their dinner. Nobody says much. We only get one chance. There's no need for me to stress the point. The tension is palpable. In my mind I run through the plan again. What's the worst that can happen? Getting caught by furious seal hunters who'd like to lynch us on the spot? Probably. Now that the pressure on the controversial seal cull is increasing globally, the clubbers are probably even more determined to silence any witnesses. I'm so glad we've got Ralph. With him on our team I know that if the worst comes to the worst we should be able to eliminate a couple of guys. I don't know about Kobe. The professional bodyguard claims to have provided protection for Nelson Mandela, but I suspect it may have been in a very distant past. He's overweight and a heavy smoker. In fact, the South African isn't fit enough to come along. But he insists, because it's what the film crew hired him for.

The first few kilometres towards the seal colony pass off without a hitch. The tide has left much of the beach damp and hard so we don't have to trudge through loose sand. The moon is in the sky, illuminating the outlines of the landscape around us. We don't need torches and our only light comes from the infrared camera that Mo switches on every now and then to film our expedition.

We take regular breaks to scan the horizon and to allow Kobe to catch his breath. The security officer is keeping up, but the first 5 of the total of 12 kilometres are beginning to take their toll. He's wheezing and needs more breathers than we'd like. Luckily for him, there's no need to rush, because it's only just after midnight and we have at least five more hours to reach our destination.

'Duck!' Ralph hisses when we're just about to get going again. He drops to his knees and presses himself against a dune. We all follow suit.

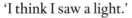

'I think I saw a light.'

We crawl up a bit and peer into the darkness.

'Over there, by that building.'

An isolated little hut, about a kilometre away and several hundred metres inland, is just about visible in the moonlight.

'Look!' Inside a lamp flashes on, and off again.

'Stay close to the ground and slip down a bit,' I whisper.

We're lying dead quiet against the eroded dunes. With our backs to the water we listen out for every little sound that's different from the murmur of the sea. Nothing. All is quiet. Ralph takes another look: the light is gone. Probably a local resident going to bed.

'We have to go past, we have no other choice,' Ralph says. 'Try to stay low to the ground, and beneath the edge of the dunes.' We all nod and walk bent-over and without a sound along the shoreline. After every step the sea fills our footprints with a thin layer of water, gradually wiping them away.

After we've covered a few hundred metres, the Australian takes his night-vision goggles and peers over the dunes again. He stares at the building.

'And?' I want to know.

'Nothing… oh, hang on… yes… yes, there is… damn… another light has flashed on. No, it's moving. It's got to be a torch. Someone's there, I'm sure.' We're too far to make out a silhouette in the dark.

'Who could it be?' Mo is keen to know.

'A security guard, a tramp, soldiers, who knows, everything is possible here,' Kobe answers. 'Perhaps the army has turned the entire Cape Cross region into an exercise area.'

'Or pure chance,' I try to put things into perspective.

'I don't know,' says Ralph, and points to a ship in the distance. The illuminated bridge inches slowly along the horizon in our direction.

'Is it…?'

'I think so.'

'Let's not all get paranoid. How could they have discovered us? I very much doubt that the person in that hut has the same quality night-vision goggles as we have. Unless the navy vessel is scanning the beach with heat sensors, we've not been seen. Let's keep an eye on that building for a while,' I suggest.

Ralph stares at the dilapidated building. All of a sudden, another light comes on.

'Somebody's coming out. That light is clearly aimed at us. How can that be?'

'Is it coming closer?'

'No, wait, a second torch has been switched on. The first one is running towards the water. No, it's going back again. Both lights are off now. The two of them are back inside,' Ralph is giving a staccato, but blood-curdling account. My heart is in my mouth. 'Now they're outside. Both of them. Oh fuck, they're running towards the sea, in our direction…'

'We've got to head back, we've got to head back,' Kobe yells. His voice is trembling and he's staring wide-eyed at the rapidly approaching light beams.

'Take it easy,' Ralph snaps at him.

I need to take control of the situation.

'Let's walk back slowly, close to the ground and through the shoreline where possible.' The team start retracing their steps back to Rosie and Dinielle, who are waiting for us 5 kilometres away, unaware of what's going on. We raise ourselves up more and more often. Ralph peers through his night-vision goggles again.

'They're walking faster,' the light beams in the distance are swinging madly to and fro.

'OK guys, run,' Ralph yells, and he starts running through the rising water. At this pace, we could be back within half an hour.

After about a kilometre we pause to catch our breath. Kobe is panting like a dog and looks ready to faint. Behind us, the lights have suddenly multiplied. 'I count five,' says Ralph.

'Five!? Where the fuck have they all come from?' I ask without really expecting an answer. The torches now march side by side on the beach. They're clearly searching for something.

Kobe wants to keep going: 'These are no tramps, no way, these are guards or the army. Come on, hurry, let's run to the road.'

'The road? Our tracks lead straight to Rosie and Dinielle – we can't abandon them.'

'They can come and pick us up. The road is closer.'

'And then what? We don't know if the police, or whoever, are there too.'

'The road. We have to get to the road.' Kobe gasps the words. He can't seem to think straight anymore. Fear is getting the better of him.

'These are real pros,' reckons Ralph, who's keeping a close eye on our pursuers. 'Let's go.'

When we turn round again Kobe has snuck off. He's staggering through the loose dune sand, trying to get to the road. Our 'guard' is not making much headway.

'The son-of-a-bitch… Kobe, Kobe!' I shout as loud as I can without revealing our position. Having covered a few dozen metres, he turns round, gesticulates and walks on. 'God damn it, what an arsehole. Well, he's on his own now. The son-of-a-bitch. Come, let's carry on along the water's edge.'

The three of us run along the beach with our gear. Ralph, who's by far the fittest thanks to his martial arts training, halts every now and then to look back and check before catching up again and reporting that they're still after us.

Somewhere halfway, I crouch down and check my mobile coverage: two bars. Let's hope they answer.

'Dinielle.'

'Pack our stuff, we're off!'

'Roger!'

That's all she needs. She can tell we're in trouble.

High on adrenaline we run the last 2 kilometres through the low beach grass and the tide line. I can only think two things: to avoid getting shot and to keep any poisonous snakes away from my calves.

The rooftop tents have been folded up and our two team members are flinging the rest of our material into the off-road vehicles. 'Go, go, go!' all three of us yell as one when we get to the cars. We can now see our pursuers. At least five of them are after us. No shots have been fired, but we're not going to wait for that to happen. Without lights, but with night-vision goggles, we tear away from our campsite and make for the main road. Ahead of us, a patrol car whizzes past in the direction of Cape Cross. It doesn't spot us.

Who were those guys by the hut? They must have received a heads-up.

'Head for the mountains.' Dinielle takes a right turn. We drive in the general direction of Swakopmund before turning into the desert towards the rocky hills. This road is far too dangerous.

The rolling landscape offers just enough cover for us to remain invisible from the road. It gives us a moment to catch our breath. Over in the distance we can see several vehicles racing up and down the normally quiet salt road. No word from Kobe.

There's only one way out: across the steep, rocky hills. Without lights.

When viewed through the night-vision goggles, the sand looks pale green, the rocks dark and the rest of the world black. We have no sense of depth or contrast. The off-road vehicle is jolted across the broken terrain and repeatedly thrown into deep potholes. Drawing on years of experience Ralph guides the cars past razor-sharp rocks and eventually, with great difficulty, to the sandy plain indicated by our GPS.

The valley is surrounded by hills and mountain ridges and makes us feel safe. At least for now. We park the Land Cruisers and swap our camouflage clothing for tourist clobber. Should anyone find us later we can always offer 'lost' as an excuse.

My phone rings. It's Tyrone, the other security guard who's with the sea team in Cape Town. He has just spoken to Kobe, who's in an abandoned mine shaft somewhere, surrounded by guards looking for him. He's trapped. Tyrone sounds furious and demands that we pick him up.

'No way,' I say. 'My priority is the safety of this team. He ran away from us, it was his decision.' Tyrone has a go at me, and keeps insisting, even though he has no idea of the situation we're in. Exasperated, I tell him that we're not doing anything and that Kobe will have to wait until the guards disappear. He'll just have to stay put for now. From where he is, it can't be much more than a couple of hundred metres to the road and the hills beyond it. As soon as he crosses those we'll pick him up. I give Tyrone our GPS coordinates, less than 500 metres as the crow flies. And Kobe should phone us, not Tyrone. After all, there's nothing they can do from Cape Town. Kobe's friend hangs up angrily, but he'll pass the message on.

But then, much to my surprise, cameraman Mo says he wants to go and collect Kobe and stalks off. Now it's my turn to fume. As long as he's on my team, I'm responsible for his safety, and I'll stop him myself if I have to. I'm not waiting for heroic Rambo shit from a cameraman who thinks he can fight his way past a horde of raging Namibians. Besides, they haven't even found Kobe yet.

Quite unexpectedly Ralph, who doesn't normally argue, takes Mo's side. He too wants to go and help Kobe. I try to explain to the group that, like them, I love the whole 'leave no man behind' ethos of the marines, but Kobe was the one who ran away. I won't jeopardise the safety of the team by pulling him out of harm's way. We'll wait here. All Kobe needs to do is lie low for a while and make his way to these coordinates. Simple. Is that clear?

Without a word, Mo rejoins the group and Ralph resigns himself to my decision.

Bobbing between hope and fear, we wait for a sign from Kobe. A couple of deep breaths help calm my thoughts. Feeling a little more relaxed, I lean against the bonnet and stare up at the clear sky over the cold desert. Billions of stars twinkle happily in the serene tranquillity of the African night. Only a howling jackal in the distance dares to disturb the peace and quiet. Even during these nail-biting moments of Operation Desert Seal the beauty of Southern Africa doesn't fail to impress me. If it weren't for the seal hunt, I'd heartily recommend this beautiful country.

My mobile vibrates on the bonnet. Kobe. He's making the call himself, which can only be good news. 'I've left the salt mine. Am about to cross the road. I'll be with you in ten minutes.'

'OK.'

We drive to the agreed location. Ten minutes turn into thirty and still no sign of Kobe. He calls again. He can't find us. Where on earth is he then? I don't fancy a discussion and give him new coordinates, not far from here.

Finally, Kobe comes staggering across a ridge. His clothes are sweat-soaked and you can tell from his face just how scared he must have been. He gives the team, including me, stiff hugs, although his eyes avoid mine. He let us down and he knows it. As far as I'm concerned, we'll never work with him again, but now is not the time to discuss this.

The story comes out in fits and starts. He feared he was done for, as armed security guards drove past repeatedly. 'They know we're around here somewhere.'

Completely shattered, he gets into the back of the four-wheel drive. 'Can we please go now?'

We get in. A return to Swakopmund is out of the question, so is staying here. Our only option is northwards from where we'll have to find a way back to capital Windhoek over the deserted roads along the Skeleton Coast.

We drive parallel to the motorway over hills and desert plains until we're far enough from Cape Cross to continue our escape over the regular salt road. Part of the Skeleton Coast has been closed off.

The roadblock boasts a skull and cross-bones and a warning sign: no entry before sunrise. Too many travellers have been overtaken by darkness, lost their way and died. There's a good reason why Portuguese explorers described this region as 'the gates to hell' when they first discovered it.

We pitch our tents in the wilderness. Exhausted, everybody falls asleep in no time. Everybody except cameraman Mo. Heartfelt swearing can be heard from his tent.

'What's wrong?' I ask.

'The footage. I didn't get any decent shots of this spectacular night. The material is worthless.'

No, it's worse than that, I think, with Captain Watson's words running through my head: unless we recorded it, it effectively never happened.

37

SPIES AND TRAITORS

Our nocturnal adventure has roused the Namibian authorities. Stories about activists in the Cape Cross region can be found in all the papers, even the national ones. The government isn't sure whether it's Sea Shepherd, but our name pops up regularly in the reports. We won't get another chance to film the cull this year. Outside opening hours, the seal reservation will be hermetically sealed by hordes of security staff, no doubt about it.

The burglary, the chases, the warships and our headlong flight through the desert: luck hasn't been on our side during this campaign. We still don't know how the pursuers on the beach got on our trail. Night-vision goggles, heat sensors, a mole in our organisation, bad luck: anything is possible.

And yet we refuse to give up. This dreadful slaughter must receive international exposure. And it's going to happen. Despite our many setbacks, we now know when the hunters start work, and we've been able to film the processing plant. Two vital tasks remain to make

Operation Desert Seal a success: a visit to the seal shop in Henties Bay and chats with the tourists at Cape Cross. For this we need everyone, so the members of the sea team join the land team in Usaku.

A visit to the shop is not without danger. The seal shop is right in the centre of Henties Bay, the stronghold of the seal hunters. But we're determined to have images of the pelts, the oil, shoes and other products made out of the Cape seals. The seals are on Appendix II of CITES, and the products may not be traded or exported without the necessary permits. The salespeople need to point this out. If they don't, they're in breach of the law. With tiny cameras concealed under their clothes Julie and Steve set off for the village to gather evidence.

Rupert and Grace drive to Cape Cross to tell tourists about the Namibian bloodbath. Vet André joins them to compare the situation before the start of the hunting season and the present, a couple of weeks later, with the cull in full swing.

The rest remain in our safe house. We're not allowed out anymore. There's a good chance we've been spotted and our descriptions have been circulated around the coastal area.

To kill time, I go online to find newspaper articles about our action at Cape Cross. It doesn't take me long: the headlines of *The Namibian* quote Bernard Esau, the Fisheries Minister, and he's not amused. 'Filming at the seal colony is illegal and absolutely unacceptable. We take this very seriously. These criminals must be brought to justice.'

Later on in the article, the chief of police reinforces the point by adding: 'These activists are violating Namibia's sovereignty. After this, what's to stop them from planting cameras in our military bases or government buildings? They're a threat to our national security and we must never yield to that.'

So now we're spies and traitors.

This man is insane, I think to myself. But we've been warned. The only positive aspect of the sensationalist reporting in the press is that the seal hunt is now national news. As long as the papers write about it, the people will talk about it. In the end they're the ones who have to demand a stop to this pointless massacre.

The initial reports from Cape Cross are encouraging. Rupert and Grace have plenty of opportunity to strike up conversations with the many foreign visitors to the sanctuary. Most are stunned to hear the true story behind the nature reserve. Nearly every tourist promises to complain to their travel organisation. Mission accomplished. And if the travel industry starts complaining too, it will be a truly giant leap towards the abolition of the hunt.

Alas, our vet doesn't have good news. The Cape seals have been decimated: abandoned pups are crawling aimlessly across the beach, crying for their mothers. Most adult females are hiding in the water with the bulls, petrified of humans loitering about the colony. The little ones wander past the occasional mother brave enough to stay on the beach. She anxiously protects her own young with her fin-feet. The small bodies drag themselves through the sand until they collapse and become fodder for the carrion birds that begin pecking tentatively at the cadavers.

André reckons thousands of seals have been slaughtered. And it will be months before the distressed animals venture back on to the beach.

A little later the team in Henties Bay call to say they're about to enter the shop. Ralph and I reckon the waiting is more nerve-racking than taking action ourselves. Less than half an hour later Julie is back on the line. They've done it, but were caught filming as they left the shop. A group of men drove after them and are slowly catching up. Steve is trying to shake them off. Could I warn Rupert?

It doesn't come as a surprise to Rupert. In fact, he's already left Cape Cross because he smelled a rat. A couple of security guards had walked towards the platform, keeping an eye on them from a distance. They hadn't seemed all that interested in the other visitors.

Julie's on the phone again. They've thrown off their pursuers, at least that's what she thinks. Steve is driving flat out to the safe house.

Immediately afterwards Rupert's on the line. Two patrol cars had just passed, their sirens wailing. They were headed for Cape Cross. Whether they're searching for us, he doesn't know, but he's stepping on the gas just to be safe.

By late afternoon, both teams arrive in Usaku. Steve shows us the pelt of a baby seal. It pains him that he had to pay for it, but at least we have the evidence we need. The saleswoman didn't mention a licence or the right paperwork or anything. 'It's all about the money,' Steve reckons, 'they don't care about the animals at all.'

Now that we've successfully completed these two tasks, we decide to return to the factory. The images we have are of poor quality. They need to be better if we're to include them in a TV documentary, the producer explains.

Our team leader hangs a map on the wall and highlights a few roads and escape routes. 'This will be our final assignment.'

'Shh, quiet,' Rupert whispers. The sound of tyres crunching on the gravel drive leading up to our house. 'Who's that?'

We all duck. A passenger car parks right outside our front door. The two dark-skinned men inside it show no sign of getting out. The man in the passenger seat is on the phone to someone and hangs up when Tyrone approaches him.

Our security guard has a brief chat with him, but I'm too far away to catch anything. After the conversation the car immediately leaves the premises.

'Something's fishy,' Tyrone says. 'They're telling me they've got a reservation for tonight. That's impossible, because we're renting the whole place. And I didn't see any luggage in the car.'

'What do you think?' Julie asks, startled.

'Reconnaissance. Those guys were sent to find us. My guess is that they've dispatched a number of teams here and there.

You've read what they're writing about us in the press. It's only a matter of time before they raid us.'

'In a word,' Steve concludes, 'we'd better get out of here.'

'That's what I'd recommend, yes,' the experienced security guard tells us.

We have no need for instructions: clothes, provisions and gear are packed and hurled into the back of the Land Cruisers. The map is taken off the wall, shredded and thrown in a skip along with other incriminating material. All traces must be removed. First off, the camera team is sent to Windhoek with all their footage. The material is essential to our operation. Then the rest get into the off-road vehicles and tear away from the safe house. Only the unmade beds suggest we were ever in Usaku.

We drive through the night to Windhoek. By now our registration numbers must be known to the police, who are clearly in cahoots with the hunters. The only thing that buys us a bit of time is the fact that the local police aren't quite as advanced as their colleagues elsewhere in the world. Even if they have a nationwide tracking system, with any luck it will be hours before our registration plates are known around the rest of the country.

In Windhoek we swap our off-road vehicles for less conspicuous rental cars after which we race to the South African border. En route we pass a couple of police checkpoints that make our breath stop short, but luckily the officers aren't looking for us. When we finally cross the border we all heave a sigh of relief. We've escaped.

38

IN CONCLUSION

Paul Watson flicks through the Namibian newspapers we brought him.

'A threat to national security,' he laughs. 'All it takes is a bit of filming.'

We're having our debriefing. We were unlucky, very unlucky, but ultimately we have good reason to be satisfied with our first campaign in Namibia, we conclude. The production team has enough suitable material to make the story of the seal hunt accessible to a large audience. And besides, nobody got caught.

'In Canada they arrest you,' Paul notes, 'here they may kill you.' And yet Sea Shepherd perseveres. Like the seal hunt in Canada and the whale hunt in Antarctica, the battle against the poachers here looks set to be a lengthy one. We'll have to keep searching for the best possible methods and latest techniques to stop these criminals in their tracks.

'Who knows, maybe we'll be able to use the ship next year,' Steve concludes, 'or maybe we should deploy drones.'

'Drones?' Watson asks.

'Yes, those unmanned airplanes with cameras.'

'Catching poachers in the act with stealth drones without being seen ourselves, I like the idea,' the former police officer in me responds eagerly. So while Paul and Steve continue their conversation, I'm already thinking about the next campaign.

In the summer of 2012 the documentary *Seal Wars* premiered. It was the first time news of the Namibian seal hunt reached an audience of millions.

EPILOGUE

There's no solution. That's to say, not one single solution. Take the seal hunt in Namibia, for instance. Our goal was to publicise the action worldwide and thereby increase pressure on the Namibian government to put a stop to the massacre. We achieved that, at least partially. After the TV documentary was broadcast Sea Shepherd received an invitation from the National Ombudsman of Namibia to join other interested parties for talks about the seal hunt so the government could investigate its legitimacy.

We received assurances that the authorities wouldn't arrest anyone. Steve Roest and I returned to give a presentation and to put forward solutions. Among them was the pledge that Sea Shepherd would invest tens of thousands of US dollars in the local economy to further develop and promote ecotourism – on the condition, of course, that the seal hunt was halted with immediate effect.

The offer was rejected. What's more, the meeting turned out to be a charade. The Ombudsman had long since decided the fate of the Cape fur seals, as it emerged a year later when his conclusion was made public. Without any kind of evidence, he argued that the hunt was legitimate and posed no danger whatsoever to the seal population. To this day, the world's biggest and cruellest mass slaughter of sea mammals takes place in Namibia.

Sea Shepherd can't stop the hunt. It can only be stopped if other non-governmental organisations, entrepreneurs, investors, governments and individuals are prepared to take a stand. The tourist sector must threaten a boycott, while the investors and entrepreneurs must come up with alternative ways of providing the impoverished seal hunters and the local population with an income. Namibia must be convinced of the economic value of the living seals, and its citizens will have to voice their concerns to the Namibian governmental agencies. The seals can only survive if a symbiosis develops between all interested parties.

Sea Shepherd is playing a small role in all this. The conservation society will continue to be at the frontline of activism. It will continue to focus on direct action, and where possible it will go after the poachers. All over the world, even as far as Antarctica.

Since the sinking of the *Ady Gil* there have been three more Antarctic campaigns: operations No Compromise, Divine Wind and Zero Tolerance. All three were extremely successful, saving the lives of hundreds of whales. In fact, during No Compromise Japan's quota was reduced by 80 per cent. A great achievement, but still not good enough. Sea Shepherd will keep going until it achieves a 100 per cent reduction.

The battle against the whale hunters will take a very long time. More than 90 per cent of the big fish have disappeared from our oceans, and nearly all fishing grounds suffer from overfishing. In fact, 95 per cent of bluefin tuna have disappeared from the Mediterranean for the simple reason that tuna makes good sushi.

Every year, tens of millions of sharks, the main predator of the sea, disappear from our waters only to end up in shark-fin soup. And although some whale species are showing signs of recovery, the number of whales swimming in the oceans today is not even 10 per cent what it was a couple of centuries ago.

If the abuse continues at this rate, it's not inconceivable that either our generation or the next will find itself living in a world in which the oceans have turned into a thick, green soup of jellyfish and algae.

Does that make me pessimistic?

No. You won't hack it on the activists' scene if you're a doom-monger. In recent years I've had the privilege of meeting many enthusiastic and passionate people who are doing something to make the world a better place. I take inspiration from their work and their ideas. Naïve? Maybe so. The battle for a healthy planet is riddled with setbacks, and only the occasional small baby step forwards. That's the reality, but I'd rather get up each morning with positive thoughts and a healthy work ethic than sulk in a corner and not lift a finger.

I have now left Sea Shepherd, and together with Steve Roest I have founded the ShadowView Foundation*, an organisation which aims to provide unmanned aerial systems, or drones, for conservation purposes and humanitarian aid. To date, these drones have been primarily deployed for military purposes, but I think we can use this great technology for the protection of man and animal alike. It can be used, for example, for tracking down poachers in Africa, for patrolling coastlines and warning swimmers about sharks, for first aid after earthquakes and for finding the whalers – plenty of possibilities.

Over the past ten years more than a thousand conservationists and park rangers have died doing their job. Most of them were murdered. Poachers will stop at nothing and are prepared to use heavy weaponry to defend their activities. I hope new technologies and other innovations will help make this important work safer.

'What can I do?' is the most frequently asked question we receive after readings or information sessions about our work. The simple answer is nothing. But even just a small gesture, like eating less fish, will make a difference. If you want to do more, you'll have to start looking for something you're passionate about. And that requires a proactive approach.

---

* www.shadowview.org

In 2010 I attended the annual meeting of the International Whaling Commission in Agadir, Morocco. Sea Shepherd was barred from the actual talks, so I was forced to report from outside the conference room. I put together a daily video blog in which I asked the delegates, among other things, why they accepted bribes or joined the Japanese delegation on their trips to the red-light district.

I spent days outside in the burning sun in the company of two surfers who happened to be in Morocco at the time. There weren't enough of us for a physical demonstration against the extermination of the whales. But what we did have was a digital counter, showing how many people had signed an anti-whaling petition online. While the delegates walked past in their expensive suits and shiny shoes without paying the slightest attention to the digital signatures, the counter crept up steadily. When the counter reached 1 million, a cardboard sign with the number was handed to one of the IWC delegates. One million people had signed the petition – a great result. Surely that merited a response? Um, no. The commission couldn't care less about the million votes. Nothing was done. The international community continues to turn a blind eye to the whale hunt.

Have a go. Try everything that makes your heart beat faster and laugh if you fail – you tried, that's what matters. And above all: don't pay too much attention to what other people say.

The Indian politician Mahatma Gandhi once said: 'Be the change that you wish to see in the world.' For many years it was my favourite quote. But now I'd like to rephrase it slightly.

Read the papers and you're likely to come across 1,001 things you want to change. There's so much misery in the world today. So much needs improving. Dwell on it too long and you'll be discouraged before you've even started. Don't be. Don't be too hard on yourself. Be a change. Just the one, somewhere, on a day when it feels right. Everything else will follow.

ACKNOWLEDGEMENTS

I could never have written this book had I not been given the chance to join the Antarctica campaign Operation Migaloo without any kind of nautical experience. My thanks to Captain Paul Watson for giving passionate volunteers the opportunity to help protect the oceans.

I'm immensely grateful to my lovely girlfriend, Andrea Schampers, who helped me put both feet firmly on the ground again and gave me the peace of mind to write.

Thanks to Wim van Gilst and Leon Verdonschot, who, without each other's knowledge, gave me the final push I needed to finally get started on this book.

Thank you to my editors Marga Deutekom and Arend Hosman of publishing company Thomas Rap. From the word go, both had the greatest faith in this project.

And of course a big thank you to Elizabeth Multon at Adlard Coles Nautical who was immediately enthused by the idea of having my book translated, and to Laura Vroomen who made it possible for you to read this book in English.

I'd like to extend a special word of thanks to my two good friends Richard van Deventer and Youssef Ait Daoud, who always cherished our friendship, whatever I did, wherever in the world and for however long.

I'm forever grateful to my dear family: my parents Theo and Ineke de Groot, Mark de Groot, Daniëlle de Groot, Marvin Siepman, Senn de Groot, Monie Broos and Karel Schampers. With an extra special thank you to my parents, who raised me with an optimistic outlook on life, and to Karel for his editorial assistance.

I'd also like to express my special thanks to all the remarkable people I've been fortunate enough to meet in the past few years and who, each in their own way, have been a source of inspiration: Phill and Trix Wollen, Rob Thielen, Ken Rutkowski, Alex Lightman, Richard Dean Anderson, Charles Hambleton, David Rosenberg, Rob Holden, Grandmaster William Cheung, Trudi Cheung, Don Schouten, Patty Mark, Amanda Duscher, Mark Sanders-Barwick, Steve and Carey Roest, Xavier Rudd, Stan Mosterd, Eric Schipper, Hesther Jolley, Hemp Hoodlamb and the men and women behind Eteam and tennis club 't Loo.

A big thank you to the indefatigable Sea Shepherd staff and the volunteers around the globe who work incredibly hard every day to keep the ships at sea. A few deserve a special mention: Wilma van Waas, Jan Hazeleger, Patrick Smeets, Anne van Ingelgem, Filip Ools, Lamya Essemlali, Darren Collins, Andrea Morello, Phyllis Clemm, Jennifer Johnson, Kelly Sullivan, Glenn and Sharra Platt, Deborah Bassett, David Hance, Susan Hartland, James Costa and Danielle Wheeler.

And finally, the incredibly brave crew and team members I was lucky enough to join on four campaigns:

Operation Migaloo: Chris Aultman, Aaron Barnes, Daniel Bebawi, Stephen Bennett, Peter Bradley, Peter Brown, Tod Emko, Robert Garcia, Jessica Gartlan, Peter Hammarstedt, Noah Hannibal, Jeff Hansen, Mal Holland, Simeon Houtman, Willie Houtman, Charles Hutchings, David Jennings, Ralph Lowe, Shannon Mann, Ian Martin, Paul Martin, Nigel Mattison, Amber Paarman, David Page, Nicola Paris, Benjamin Potts, Zin Rain, Stephen Sikes, Alex Wallman and Paul Watson.

Operation Musashi: Chris Aultman, Simon Avery, Daniel Bebawi, Peter Brown, Damien Byrne, Eric Cheng, Laura Dakin, Arne Feuerhahn, Josh Gunn, Peter Hammarstedt, Jeff Hansen,

Mal Holland, Willie Houtman, Emily Hunter, Charles Hutchings, Don Kehoe, Molly Kendall, Veronika Kristoff, Adam Lau, Shannon Mann, Pedro Montero, David Nickarz, Amber Paarman, Andrew Perry, Benjamin Potts, Zin Rain, Merry Redenbach, Richard Roberts, Steve Roest, Jane Taylor, Doug Tompkins, Wietse van der Werf, Luke Van Horn, Dan Villa, Paul Watson and Warren Werrett.

Operation Waltzing Matilda, the *Ady Gil* crew: Pete Bethune, James Burrowes, Mike Smith, Jason Stewart and cameraman Simeon Houtman.

Operation Desert Seal: Julie Anderson, Nikki Botha, Ralph Herde, Rupert Imhoff, Grace Ko, Kobe, Rosie Kunneke, Tyron Kupritz, Andre Menache, Steve Roest, Dinielle Stöckigt and *Seal Wars* producer Anthony Sacco.

GLOSSARY

Butyric acid – a biodegradable and extremely smelly substance, which is neither toxic nor corrosive. Butyric acid can be found in, among other things, rancid butter, sweat and many strong-smelling cheeses. The Sea Shepherd activists hurl bottles of the substance on to the whalers' decks to taint the whale meat and stop the hunters from working.

Delta – an inflatable rubber dinghy with two outboard motors. The dinghy, which was one of two on board the *Steve Irwin*, can seat four. Maximum speed: 30 knots.

Gemini – an inflatable rubber dinghy with two outboard motors. The six-seat dinghy was kept on board the *Steve Irwin*. After Operation Musashi, it was so badly damaged it could no longer be deployed. Maximum speed: 40 knots.

The Institute of Cetacean Research – an organisation claiming to carry out research into whales. The institute is government-subsidised and charters a number of vessels in the whale hunt around Antarctica.

Knot – a unit expressing the speed of vessels or the wind, corresponding to 1 sea mile (1.8 kilometres) per hour.

LRAD – Long Range Acoustic Device, a sonic cannon which emits high or low frequencies with the aim of dispersing or disorientating people. A weapon used by the Japanese whalers.

M/Y *Ady Gil* – a 24-metre trimaran, built in a style that allowed it to pierce the waves as it were, hence the name wave-piercer. Under its original name, *Earthrace*, it broke the world record for circumnavigating the globe on biodiesel. It was renamed after a donation by entrepreneur Ady Gil and deployed by Sea Shepherd in Antarctica in 2009. The organisation hoped that its speed would help them locate the whaling fleet as quickly as possible. Maximum speed: 40 knots.

M/Y *Bob Barker* – a former Norwegian whaler built in 1950. Sea Shepherd bought the ship in 2009 after a $5 million donation by American TV personality Bob Barker. The ship was first deployed during Operation Waltzing Matilda and was strong enough to navigate through ice. Maximum speed: 18 knots.

M/Y *Steve Irwin* – the Sea Shepherd flagship. The nearly 60-metre ship was built in 1975 and formerly served as a Scottish patrol vessel. In 2007 Sea Shepherd renamed it the *Steve Irwin*, in honour of the conservationist and crocodile hunter who died in 2006. Maximum speed: 16.5 knots.

Nisshin Maru – the factory ship of the Japanese whaling fleet, weighing 8,000 tonnes and measuring 130 metres. Harpoon vessels transport shot whales to the ship, where they are then cut up and processed. Maximum speed: 15.5 knots.

Paul Watson (born 1950) – Canadian environmental and animal rights activist. He is the founder and chairman of the Sea Shepherd Conservation Society and has worked as a captain on the Sea Shepherd vessels for over 35 years.

Prop fouler – a long, thick piece of rope, usually reinforced with Kevlar or iron wire. The prop fouler is thrown into the water, in front of a ship's bow, in the hope that it will wrap itself around the propeller and propeller shaft, preventing the ship from continuing.

Sea Shepherd Conservation Society – an international environmental organisation, founded in 1977 with the aim of protecting all marine wildlife. Sea Shepherd's mission is to end the slaughter of marine life and the destruction of their habitat in order to conserve and protect ecosystems and species.

The organisation uses direct action to expose and confront illegal activities at sea.

Shonan Maru 2 – a former Japanese harpoon vessel converted into a security vessel to protect the whaling fleet. The harpoon was replaced with a water cannon. In 2010, the vessel was involved in the collision with the *Ady Gil*. Maximum speed: approximately 22 knots.

Whale Wars – a television series documenting Sea Shepherd's campaigns against Japan's whaling activities in Antarctica. In the US the show is broadcast on Animal Planet, in the UK on the Discovery Channel.

Yushin Maru 1, 2 and *3* – Japanese harpoon vessels operating in the waters around the South Pole. Maximum speed: approximately 22 knots.